SEASONS OF LIFE
FACULTY MANUAL AND TEST BANK

by

Richard O. Straub
University of Michigan-Dearborn

From
The Annenberg/CPB Collection

Seasons of Life Faculty Manual and Test Bank
by Richard O. Straub

This *Faculty Manual/Test Bank* is part of a full college course, which also includes five one-hour television programs; 26 half-hour audio programs; *The Developing Person Through the Life Span,* second edition, by Kathleen Stassen Berger (Worth Publishers, Inc.) and a Study Guide. For information about licensing the course, purchasing video and audiocassettes or course print components, call 1-800-LEARNER, or write the Annenberg/CPB Project, P.O. Box 1922, Santa Barbara, CA 93116–1922.

Other materials based on **Seasons of Life** include 20 six-minute audio modules, and a companion book, **Seasons of Life,** by John Kotre and Elizabeth Hall (Little, Brown and Company). The book is available by calling 1-800-LEARNER and in most bookstores.

Funding for **Seasons of Life** is provided by the Annenberg/CPB Project.

ISBN: 0–87901–472–5
Printing: 4   3   2   1   Year: 93   92   91   90

Preface

Seasons of Life is one-semester, college-level telecourse in life-span development. To present the many dimensions of this fascinating topic, our staff at the University of Michigan and WQED-TV/Pittsburgh has culled the insights of nearly seventy-five leading reasearchers in several academic disciplines, including developmentalists, psychologists, sociologists, geneticists, and anthropologists, and recorded significant events in the lives of more than one hundred people. The result is an exploration—from both the expert and the personal perspectives—of human development beginning with conception and continuing through the many changes of growth and aging.

The course includes five components: (1) five one-hour video programs designed for broadcast over public television stations; (2) twenty-six half-hour audio programs; (3) a text—*The Developing Person Through the Life Span, second edition,* by Kathleen Stassen Berger; (4) a *Study Guide* to help students integrate the various components of the course; and (5) this *Faculty Manual and Test Bank,* which includes ideas for teaching this course and a bank of multiple-choice and essay questions. The materials of the telecourse are organized into twenty-six lessons, which can be adjusted to suit many different course plans (see page ix).

The ***Seasons of Life*** telecourse has been designed to:

Introduce the theory, methods, and research findings of life-span development.

Communicate the insights that psychologists, biologists, sociologists, and anthropologists have contributed to our understanding of human development.

Describe how the biological, social, and psychological "clocks" influence the events of the life cycle.

Stimulate students to be active learners. Each lesson contains an exercise that encourages students to reflect on their own lives or to better understand others'. At the end of the course, a Television Term Project calls on students to interpret examples from their own life experiences in view of what they have learned from the telecourse.

Encourage student-teacher interaction. Student exercises and the Television Term Project provide instructors with a stream of information about students' knowledge, views, and experiences. Such feedback can help instructors to improve communication with their students and may even generate research ideas.

Develop an understanding of how life stories evolve from childhood to old age and, in the process, motivate students to formulate and reflect on their own life stories and those of others.

THE TELECOURSE

The *Seasons of Life* telecourse and its five components are organized by topics within a broader chronological framework.

The Television Programs

The video component of **Seasons of Life** is a five-part television series produced by WQED/Pittsburgh for the Public Broadcasting Service. Each of the five one-hour programs uses life histories to introduce students to the major themes of a particular period of life. Program One introduces the "clocks" that influence biological, social, and psychological development throughout life and explores development during the first six years. Program Two covers development during childhood and adolescence (ages 6–20) and Program Three looks at early adulthood (ages 20–40). Programs Four and Five focus on middle adulthood (ages 40–60) and late adulthood (ages 60+), respectively.

The television programs are hosted by David Hartman, formerly of ABC's "Good Morning, America." Each program tells the story of human development through the voices of people in all seasons of life and through the commentary of researchers who study the life span. The television programs are central to the Television Term Project.

The Audio Programs

The audio component of the telecourse is a series of twenty-six half-hour programs, each exploring a special topic related to one of the twenty-six lessons of the telecourse. The audio programs—introduced by David Hartman and hosted by John Kotre, a psychologist specializing in life narratives—form the basis of day-to-day work in the **Seasons of Life** telecourse.

The Textbook

The textbook for the course is *The Developing Person Through the Life Span, second edition,* by Kathleen Stassen Berger, published by Worth Publishers. Organized into twenty-six chapters, each with a related audio program, this text provides the general framework for the telecourse. Within a chronological perspective, the textbook covers infancy, the play years, the school years, adolescence, early adulthood, middle adulthood, and late adulthood. For each stage, separate chapters cover physical, cognitive, and psychosocial development. An engaging writing style, clear organization, helpful pedagogy, up-to-date research, and practical applications have contributed to the textbook's popularity with instructors and students.

The Study Guide

The *Seasons of Life Study Guide* was written by Richard O. Straub and published by Worth Publishers. The *Study Guide* integrates the elements of the telecourse and provides students with a step-by-step program for meeting the telecourse objectives. The *Study Guide* is organized by lessons that parallel the audio programs and the textbook. Each lesson contains an orientation, a statement of lesson goals, audio and textbook assignments, and a set of questions for student self-testing.

Especially important are the short exercises in each lesson that encourage active learning by guiding students to make connections between the content of the course and their own life experiences. Students complete these exercises and return them to their instructor. The *Study Guide* concludes with a Television Term Project consisting of essay questions keyed to the video programs. The questions encourage students to integrate what they have learned about life-span development and to relate their knowledge to their own experiences and observations.

Another feature of the *Study Guide,* titled "How to Use Your Time Effectively and Study More Efficiently," contains many suggestions for helping students to improve their study skills. A student study guide for the Berger textbook is published separately by Worth Publishers.

The Faculty Manual and Test Bank

This telecourse *Faculty Manual and Test Bank* provides background on **Seasons of Life,** suggests course plans, and offers hints for teaching this course effectively.

Suggestions are given for evaluating and providing feedback for each student exercise and the Television Term Project. Each chapter of the manual also contains a test bank of fifteen multiple-choice questions and ten essay questions. The multiple-choice questions cover material from the audio programs only. The essay questions cover material from both the textbook and the audio programs. A test bank for the Berger textbook is published separately by Worth Publishers.

ACKNOWLEDGMENTS

We are grateful to everyone who has contributed to this project. Special thanks go to our core group of advisors: Urie Bronfenbrenner of Cornell University, David Gutmann of Northwestern University, Bernice Neugarten of the University of Chicago, Anne Petersen of Penn State University, Alice Rossi of the University of Massachusetts–Amherst, and Sheldon White of Harvard University. Jack Mitchell of WHA at the University of Wisconsin provided much wise counsel regarding audio programming. Janet Whitaker of Rio Salado Community College was especially helpful in the design of our supplementary materials. Margie Moeller of WQED wrote excellent descriptions of the people in the television programs. Wilbert McKeachie and Elizabeth Douvan of the University of Michigan offered help close to home, and the staff of Worth Publishers supplied both patience and professionalism. Major funding for **Seasons of Life** was provided by the Annenberg/CPB Project.

In preparing the materials that make up the **Seasons of Life** project, we were guided by a simple idea: that by examining the stories people tell about their lives, we can come to an understanding not only of these lives but of the life cycle itself, and of its "seasons." We hope the telecourse experience will be an interesting and enjoyable one for you and your students.

John Kotre, Ph.D.
Professor of Psychology
   University of Michigan–Dearborn
Project Director, *Seasons of Life*

Richard O. Straub, Ph.D.
Associate Professor of Psychology
   University of Michigan–Dearborn

Table of Contents

Planning the Seasons of Life Telecourse

The nontraditional students who are most likely to take telecourses are likely to be older than residential students. Thus, they tend to be married, employed full or part time, and raising families. Students' reasons for enrolling in the *Seasons of Life* telecourse will be diverse. They may want to understand their own developmental past, present, and future; they may want to know how to raise their children or care for their aging parents; or they may be preparing for careers working with people of a specific age. Knowing your students' interests and goals will help you choose the most appropriate course plan (some examples follow). One way to obtain the information is to include a return-requested postcard in your introductory letter to students (see page xv).

THE BASIC PLAN

Each *Seasons of Life* lesson consists of an audio program and a chapter in the text and *Study Guide.* You may require students to take a quiz on these materials and/or to complete the written exercises in the *Study Guide.*

In a semester of thirteen weeks, these lessons can be scheduled at the rate of two per week (Schedule A). the pace of these lessons can be adjusted to accommodate terms of other lengths.

Week	Schedule A—The Basic Plan
1	Lessons 1 and 2
2	3 and 4
3	5 and 6
4	7 and 8
5	9 and 10
6	11 and 12
7	13 and 14
8	15 and 16
9	17 and 18
10	19 and 20
11	21 and 22
12	23 and 24
13	25 and 26
	Television Term Project

If the time available in a semester does not allow coverage of all the lessons, there are several options. You may reduce the requirements for each lesson, omitting either the quiz or the exercise. Your choice of activities will give the course either a traditional flavor or a more experiential one. The latter may be particularly suited to the cognitive strengths of older students. You may reduce the number of lessons, giving your course a biological, cognitive, or psychosocial emphasis, or stressing certain periods of the life span. The organization of the telecourse makes it easy to eliminate a section or sections, such as middle adulthood (Lessons 20, 21, 22) or late adulthood (Lessons 23, 24, 25), without interfering with the integrity of the content. However, if you decide not to assign these lessons, you might suggest that students listen to the telecourse programs and read the corresponding chapters of the textbook after the course is over.

ALTERNATIVE PLANS

If your students are preparing for a specific career, you may wish to emphasize certain aspects of development. Nursing students, for example, would benefit from the material on biological development and on coping with critical transitions (Schedule B).

Week	Schedule B—For Nursing Students
1	Lesson 1
2	Lessons 3 and 4
3	5
4	7 and 8
5	11
6	14 and 15
7	16
8	17 and 18
9	19
10	20 and 21
11	22
12	23 and 24
13	26
	Television Term Project

Instructors in departments of family studies and home economics may prefer an emphasis on psychosocial development, as in Schedule C.

Week	Schedule C—For Students in Family Studies and Home Economics Programs
1	Lesson 1
2	Lessons 3 and 4
3	7
4	10 and 11
5	13
6	14 and 15
7	16
8	17 and 18
9	19
10	20 and 21
11	22
12	24 and 25
13	26
	Television Term Project

Students preparing for teaching careers require knowledge of childhood and adolescence and on cognitive development throughout the entire life span (Schedule D).

Week	Schedule D—For Students in Education Programs
1	Lesson 1
2	Lessons 2 and 6
3	7
4	8 and 9
5	10
6	11 and 12
7	13
8	14 and 15
9	16
10	18 and 19
11	21
12	22 and 24
13	26
	Television Term Project

Another possibility is teaching *Seasons of Life* over two semesters. In this design, one lesson per week would be appropriate (Schedule E).

Week, Semester One	Schedule E—Two-Semester Course
1	Lesson 1
2	2
3	3
4	4
5	5
6	6
7	7
8	8
9	9
10	10
11	11
12	12
13	13

Week, Semester Two	
1	Lesson 14
2	15
3	16
4	17
5	18
6	19
7	20
8	21
9	22
10	23
11	24
12	25
13	26
	Television Term Project

THE STUDENT-PLANNED COURSE

Another telecourse plan gives students the option of configuring the course according to their own goals and interests. In this approach, students choose both their course emphasis and their preferred style of learning.

First, students select *what* they wish to learn. They may stress particular stages of life or certain domains of development that are relevant to their family, their friends, their work, and ultimately to themselves. Instructors may impose some constraints on the selection of lessons in order to ensure that the life-span integrity of the course is maintained.

Second, students choose *how* they wish to learn. Some may opt for quizzes and examinations; others, for the open-ended exercises and the Television Term Project; still others, for a combination of the two. In this way, students of different ages and varying levels of college experience can build on their particular intellectual strengths.

For a student-designed telecourse, instructors may develop a point-based grading system such as the following: A = 1000 or more points, B = 900 or more points, C= 800 or more points, D = 700 or more points.
By successfully completing any combination of examinations and exercises, each of which is assigned a specific point value, students work toward their individual goals. A sample record-keeping grid that will facilitate this approach is provided in the "Supplementary Materials" section of this Faculty Manual. A similar grid appears in the student Study Guide.

ASSIGNMENTS AND EXAMINATIONS

The manner in which students complete telecourse assignments and exams will vary according to the way telecourses are offered at your institution. Generally, students feel that regular assignments, such as the quizzes and exercises which appear in the *Seasons of Life Study Guide*, are beneficial. They encourage students to keep up with the course work and provide frequent reinforcement of subject material.

Quizzes based on the audio material can be developed from the telecourse test bank in this manual. Both multiple-choice and essay questions are provided. A test bank for the textbook, *The Developing Person Through The Life Span, 2/e*, is published separately by Worth Publishers, Inc. Quizzes can be mailed to students on a regular basis, returned to your institution for scoring (possibly by computer), with the results mailed back to the students.

Lengthier unit, mid-term, and final exams can also be developed from the course's testbanks. Administering these exams may present something of a challenge because not all students will be able to attend an on-campus examination at a particular hour. One arrangement practiced successfully by a number of colleges is to schedule two periods for testing (Friday evening and Sunday afternoon, for example). Some instructors also divide the two periods between two locations, one on-campus and one downtown in a public library or civic center that might be convenient for students.

Some colleges have exam centers, staffed by paraprofessionals, daytime, evening, and weekend hours that are ideally suited for telecourses. Students may choose the most convenient hour and day to be tested (within a range of one week, for example).

The Television Term Project, found in the Study Guide, is to be completed, then either mailed or brought in by students at the time of the final examination.

THE INSTRUCTOR'S ROLE

The particulars of syllabus, assignments, classroom meetings, and tests for your telecourse will naturally vary from situation to situation. Factors that might affect the instructor's role include: your institution's course requirements and definition of instructor responsibilities; the level at which the course is being offered (upper or lower division, number of credits); the extent to which you choose to shape the course to reflect specific goals and areas of specialization; student needs, including work loads and travel.

There are many options for managing the telecourse. For example, the instructor can be a course manager responsible primarily for organizing a course syllabus, sending materials to students, receiving and evaluating assignments, grading examinations, and responding to student questions, as needed. This role would be especially appropriate for students who are highly independent learners.

The instructor can also play a more active role in initiating interaction with and among students. In this role, the instructor could also become tutor, discussion leader, and mentor to students. This can be done even when on-campus sessions are kept to a minimum or made optional. This approach is especially appropriate for students who, although self-motivated, find that they need some external direction as well as opportunities to interact with fellow students.

Depending on the role they adopt, instructors may be responsible for some of the following tasks.

Before the Telecourse

- Review the course objectives, components, and suggestions for planning the course.

- Set up administrative and academic policies and procedures that will govern the course offering (e.g., curricular placement, course number, number of credits, grading policy with specific requirements, the number and type of exams.)

- Identify the type and level of services which will be available to you as the course instructor and to your students.

- Adjust assignments to ensure that the course meets your institutions's requirements for academic credit or to "customize" the course as you see fit.

- Write a course description for use in course catalogs and class schedules.

- Prepare a course syllabus that informs students of course requirements, due dates, grading policies, television broadcast times, tape availability on campus, office hours, and methods for making personal contact (a sample is provided in the "Supplementary Materials" section of this manual, page xv.)

- Decide whether on-campus meetings will be offered and, if so, whether they will be optional or required.

- Verify that the bookstore has ordered sufficient copies of *The Developing Person Through The Life Span, 2/e,* by Kathleen Stassen Berger (Worth Publishers, Inc.).

During the Telecourse

Experience has shown that telecourse students generally are highly motivated. However, telecourses often attract students unfamiliar with college instruction, as well as those who have completed college-level work but are unfamiliar with distant learning and independent study. To reduce possible student anxiety and promote communication with students, the faculty member might:

- Prepare and send an introductory letter to students (suggested content is provided in the "Supplementary Materials" section of this manual, page xv.)

- Offer an orientation session for students.

- Preview each television and audio program and review each component of all telecourse lessons (textbook chapter, Study Guide, Faculty Manual).

- Consider developing regular "newsletters" for distribution throughout the course to remind students of due dates, events, and assignments.

- Schedule optional on-campus sessions to provide students with opportunities to exchange views and ask questions.

- Encourage students to submit Study Guide exercises on time.

- Promptly provide feedback to students on their Study Guide exercises and other assignments.

- Hold review sessions before mid-term and final examinations.

- If necessary, establish special test sites.

After the Telecourse

- Have students complete a course evaluation.

- Assign final grades and see that they are forwarded to the appropriate office.

- Return student work and projects, if appropriate.

- Evaluate the telecourse experience; note any adjustments to be made to future offerings of the telecourse.

SUPPLEMENTARY MATERIALS

Checklist of Responsibilities

	Target Date	Date Completed
Review Faculty Manual	————	————
Order desk copies of print materials	————	————
Confirm reservation of facilities	————	————
Prepare schedule of assignments, meetings, phone and office hours	————	————
Verify that bookstore has ordered text and Study Guide	————	————
Confirm that library or media center has copies of telecourse materials	————	————
Verify final broadcast schedule	————	————
Prepare and mail welcome letter	————	————
Prepare and distribute course syllabus	————	————
Notify students about seminars and other meetings	————	————
Establish special test sites	————	————
Contact students who appear to be inactive	————	————
Provide regular feedback to students on their course progress	————	————
Prepare and deliver mid-term exam notices	————	————
Prepare and mail mid-term exams	————	————
Grade mid-term exams and notify students of results	————	————
Schedule make-up exams	————	————
Notify students of final exam	————	————
Administer final exam	————	————
Complete final make-up exams	————	————
Prepare and distribute course evaluation	————	————
Grade final exams, determine grades, notify students, submit grades	————	————
Evaluate the course	————	————

Suggestions for Introductory Letter

It is advisable to send an introductory letter to students as soon as their registration forms have been accepted. The letter can describe the course in greater detail and might include the following:

- a description of course components, including the textbook and The Study Guide and where they can be purchased;

- a sequence of lessons;

- a broadcast schedule, including the availability of tapes on campus for review;

- scheduled times and locations of course-related activities, such as discussion groups and examinations;

- course requirements and grading policies;

- campus services available to students, including library and media center hours;

- name, telephone number, and office hours of the instructor;

- a return-requested postcard with space for students to indicate their reasons or special interests in taking the course.

Sample Syllabus

> Course:
> Instructor:

Course Description

> *Seasons of Life* is an introductory telecourse that explores human development from the beginning of life to the end. A major theme is that the course of life is governed by three developmental "clocks" that pace the biological, social, and psychological changes in the individual.
>
> The development of the individual is an exciting process, beginning with the rapid metamorphoses of cells at conception and continuing through the intricate changes of growth and aging. The study of the life span is also intriguing because each of us, and everyone we care about, is constantly developing.
>
> The telecourse consists of twenty-six lessons including television and audio programs accompanied by a Study Guide and textbook. The Study Guide contains the "recipe" that will direct you, step-by-step, through each of the lessons of the telecourse. In completing the telecourse, you will write and send in assignments based on exercises in the Study Guide, take examinations, and complete a Television Term Project that incorporates all components of the telecourse.

Textbook and Study Guide

> Two books are necessary for the course and may be purchased at the college bookstore:
>
> Text: Kathleen Stassen Berger, *The Developing Person Through the Life Span, 2/e.* New York: Worth Publishers Inc.
>
> Study Guide: Richard O. Straub. *Study Guide to Accompany Seasons of Life.* New York: Worth Publishers Inc.

Instructor/Consultant

> Your instructor will be available in his or her office for phone consultations for three hours each week, and at other times by appointment. You will receive, from the instructor, an introductory letter of available times for phone consultation and other procedures.

Evaluation

> The final course grade will be a weighted average of the following: all student exercises: _____%, all quizzes _____%, midterm exam _____%, final exam _____%, Television Term Project _____%.

Written Assignments

All written assignments are contained in the Study Guide. Your instructor will send you a calendar for mail-in assignments and due dates.

Exams will cover both the textbook and programs. The format of the exams will be multiple choice, short answer, and essay, and each exam will last approximately one hour. The final exam will be cumulative and draw from all material that has been covered in the course.

Policies   There will be no make-up exams without a medical excuse or permission by the instructor given at least one week prior to the exam. Assignments are expected on time, and late assignments will receive lower scores.

Schedule of Readings, Assignments, and Telecourse Programs

Week One:

Week Two:

etc.

Sample Record-Keeping Grid

Student name _____

Student number _____

Lesson	Exercise Score	Quiz Score
1		
2		
3		
4		
5		
6		
7		
8		
9		
10		
11		
12		
13		
14		
15		
16		
17		
18		
19		
20		
21		
22		
23		
24		
25		
26		
Total		

Average _____

Exercise average _____

Quiz average _____

Mid-term exam _____

Final exam _____

Television term project _____

Overall average _____

Final grade _____

Introduction

AUDIO PROGRAM: Of Seasons, Stories, and Lives

OVERVIEW

Lesson 1 of *Seasons of Life* introduces students to the field of developmental psychology and identifies several themes emphasized throughout the series. The first reflects the emerging **life-span perspective,** according to which development is viewed as a life-long process not confined to any one period, or "season," of life.

A second theme of the series is that three **developmental clocks** play a role in each season of life. The **biological clock** is a metaphor for the body's way of timing physical development. The **social clock** reflects society's age norms for when certain life events should occur. The **psychological clock** represents each person's inner timetable for development.

Lesson 1 also describes the methods of developmental research, including **naturalistic observation, case studies, interviews,** and **experimentation.** In Chapter 1 of *The Developing Person Through the Life Span, 2/e,* author Kathleen Berger discusses the strengths and weakness of each method and two continuing controversies. These are the **nature-nurture** issue regarding the relative importance of biological (nature) and environmental (nurture) influences on development, and the question of whether development is best viewed as a **continuous process** or a sequence of distinct **stages.**

Audio Program 1, "Of Seasons, Stories, and Lives," introduces a third theme of the series by noting that the methods of developmental research also include the interpretation of **life stories.** During the program we hear several people recall their earliest memories and memories of **nuclear episodes**—the most significant scenes in their stories. Through the expert commentary of psychologists Dan McAdams and Richard Lerner, students learn what such **autobiographical memories** mean and how research is done from the life-span perspective.

LESSON GOALS

1. To define developmental psychology and explain the life-span and the ecological perspectives.

2. To describe the various research methods used by developmental psychologists, noting the strengths and weaknesses of each.

3. To discuss the significance of the three developmental clocks through the life span.

4. To explain how the interpretation of life stories and autobiographical memories helps psychologists to understand development through the life span.

LESSON 1 EXERCISE: FIRST MEMORIES

The exercise for Lesson 1 focuses on the concept of autobiographical memory and its usefulness to developmental psychologists attempting to understand an individual's life story. Students are asked to reflect on the first memories of individuals in the audio program and to describe their own earliest memory, or that of someone they know. This exercise introduces an important aspect of exercises in later lessons in that it encourages students to make meaningful connections between the lesson's material and their own experiences.

    As a way of providing feedback to students, the instructor might note whether students' answers to the first two questions in the exercise accurately reflect audio program content.

1. How did Mary's first memory relate to the rest of her life story? How did it express her identity?

   Mary's earliest memory was of crying as she watched her mother walk away from her. Whether or not this memory is accurate (Mary's mother doesn't remember the incident), it reflects a fear of disapproval that has been a dominant theme throughout Mary's life.

2. How did Arnelle Douglas' first memory relate to the rest of his life story? How did it express his identity?

   Arnelle Douglas' earliest memory was of lying sick in bed, waiting for his father to take him to the hospital. Arnelle's pain and anger at being rejected by his father throughout most of his childhood is reflected in his determination to be a better father to his own children—to be the father that appears in his first memory.

The third question asks students to integrate the material from the audio program with their life experiences.

3. Of course, not all first memories relate to the rest of a person's story. Ask someone you know (or yourself) his or her earliest memory. Do you see any connection between the memory and the rest of the person's life story? Between the memory and your subject's sense of who he or she is?

   Since there is no correct or incorrect answer to this question, the most appropriate feedback might be a general statement regarding the significance of earliest memories to the life story and to identity.

AUDIO TESTBANK

Note: A testbank for the text is published separately by Worth Publishers, Inc.

Multiple Choice Questions

The correct answer to each question is identified by a capital letter.

1. According to a new perspective in developmental psychology, you can't understand the young without understanding the old. And you can't understand young or old people without understanding everyone else in between. This is called the:
   a. systems perspective.
   b. ecological perspective.
   C. life-span perspective.
   d. continuity perspective.

2. Which of the following is an example of longitudinal research?
   a. An investigator compares the performance of several different age groups on a test of memory.
   B. The performance of the same group of people on a test of memory is compared at several different ages.
   c. The performance of an experimental group and a control group of subjects on a test of memory is compared.
   d. The performance of several different age groups of subjects on a test of memory is compared as each group is tested repeatedly over a period of years.

3. The social clock represents:
   a. a person's inner timetable for development.
   b. the body's mechanisms of timing development.
   c. that point in each individual's life when the need to be accepted by others is especially strong.
   D. society's standards, or age norms, for when certain life events should happen.

4. The concept of the psychological clock emphasizes which of the following?
   A. Each individual plays an active role in his or her development.
   b. Each person's development is strongly influenced by the particular historical events of their own birth cohort.
   c. Development is most diverse early in life and becomes more similar from person to person during later seasons.
   d. Each person's sense of identity is strongly determined by the bodily changes that occur at different ages.

5. Most people report their earliest memory occurring at about age:
   a. 1 or 2.
   B. 3 or 4.
   c. 5 or 6.
   d. 7 or 8.

6. Memories of especially significant moments in life are examples of:
    A. nuclear episodes.
    b. semantic memories.
    c. network memories.
    d. episodic memories.

7. Earliest memories are typically:
    a. quite accurate and factual.
    b. inaccurate and fictitious.
    C. mixtures of reality and fantasy.
    d. based on unemotional sensory impressions.

8. According to experts on the audio program, earliest memories are often:
    A. a preview of an important theme in an individual's life story.
    b. of little significance in an individual's life story.
    c. more vivid in women than in men.
    d. more vivid in men than in women.

9. Remembering the best moment in your life is an example of a(n):
    a. flashbulb memory.
    B. nuclear episode.
    c. foundation memory.
    d. episodic memory.

10. Professor McAdams believes that people are likely to reveal their personality traits when they:
    a. describe everyday events in their lives.
    B. recount significant moments in their life stories.
    c. speculate about who they will be in the future.
    d. a and b.

11. The timing of birth, growth, fertility, and death, is governed by the:
    A. biological clock.
    b. social clock.
    c. psychological clock.
    d. interaction of the three developmental clocks.

12. In the United States today, the social clock:
    a. is set just about where it was at the turn of the century.
    b. has its greatest influence on people of lower socioeconomic status.
    c. no longer is an important influence on development.
    D. is set very differently than it was fifty years ago.

13. The idea that development continues throughout life rather than being restricted to one season:
    a. has been a central tenet of developmental psychology since its inception.
    B. is a relatively new perspective in developmental psychology.
    c. is widely disputed.
    d. a and c are correct.

14. According to the audio program, development is governed by which three "clocks"?
    a. emotional, intellectual, physical
    b. physical, cognitive, psychosocial
    C. biological, social, psychological
    d. physical, emotional, intellectual

15. According to the audio program, human development is most diverse during:
    a. infancy.
    b. childhood.
    c. adolescence.
    D. adulthood.

Essay Questions

1. Explain the "life-span perspective" in developmental psychology and the concept that there are "seasons" of life. (audio program)

2. Compare and contrast the three developmental clocks. (audio program)

3. Explain the significance of first memories and nuclear episodes in the interpretation of life stories. (audio program)

4. Identify and discuss two major areas of controversy in developmental psychology today. (text)

5. Cite the steps usually involved in applying the scientific method. (text)

6. Describe the major research methods used by developmental psychologists and cite the strengths and weaknesses of each method. (text)

7. Compare and contrast longitudinal, cross-sectional, and sequential research methods. (text)

8. Tell how the settings of the three developmental clocks differ for someone in your generation, your parents' generation, and someone younger than yourself, such as a child, niece, or nephew. (audio program and text)

9. Describe your earliest memory or that of a nuclear episode from your early years. In what ways does this memory relate to the rest of your life story? In what ways is it an expression of your identity? (audio program and text)

10. The textbook describes the ecological approach to studying development. Give an example of a research topic for which this approach would be best suited and explain your reasoning. (text)

References

Neugarten, B. L. (1985). Interpretive social science and research on aging. In Alice S. Rossi (ed.) *Gender and the life course*, New York: Aldine Publishing Co., pp. 291-300.

Professor Neugarten, an eminent sociologist who provides expert commentary in the *Seasons of Life* television series, makes a persuasive argument that the research methods of the natural sciences are of limited use in the study of life-span development.

Rubin, D. C. (1985). The subtle deceiver: recalling our past. *Psychology Today.* (September), pp. 39-46.

Professor Rubin discusses research on autobiographical memory and the insights it yields into each person's sense of him or herself.

Theories

AUDIO PROGRAM: The Story of Erik Erikson

OVERVIEW

Lesson 1 introduced the subject matter of developmental psychology, described three clocks that govern development, and explained the various research methods of life-span psychology. Lesson 2 deals with theories of human development, one of which is Erik Erikson's psychosocial approach and the subject of the audio program.

Chapter 2 of the textbook compares and evaluates four of those theories that have significantly influenced life-span psychology: **psychoanalytic theory, learning theory, cognitive theory,** and **humanistic theory.** Author Kathleen Berger notes most developmental psychologists today take an **eclectic** perspective, applying insights from various theories rather than limiting themselves to only one school of thought.

Among the psychoanalytic theorists, Erik Erikson was one of the first to devote attention to the entire life cycle—to adulthood as well as to childhood. He departed from the viewpoint of his mentor Sigmund Freud, by perceiving a more significant influence of social and cultural factors in development. Erikson proposed eight psychosocial stages, each of which centers on an important developmental **crisis.** In the audio program, Erikson describes his early experiences in Germany and America and how he came to create one of psychology's most influential theories of the life cycle.

LESSON GOALS

1. To explain the role theories play in developmental psychology.

2. To outline the basic terms and themes of the four major theories of human development: psychoanalytic theory, learning theory, humanistic theory, and cognitive theory.

3. To discuss the eclectic perspective in developmental psychology.

4. To describe Erikson's eight stages of psychosocial development and discuss the significance of Erikson's theory in life-span psychology.

LESSON 2 EXERCISE: THEORIES OF HUMAN DEVELOPMENT

To help clarify their understanding of the similar, contradictory, and comple-mentary aspects of the major developmental theories, the student exercise for Lesson 2 asks students to answer the following questions. Since this exercise is straightforward, the most appropriate feedback from instructor to students is a listing of the correct answers, which are given below following each question.

1. Which of the major developmental theories are stage theories? Which are not?

   Psychoanalytic and cognitive theories are stage theories; learning and humanistic theories are not. Maslow's hierarchy of needs does not represent stages, but rather individual circumstances.

2. Which theories emphasize individual conscious organization of experience? Unconscious urges? Observable behavior? Individuality?

   Cognitive theories emphasize individual conscious organization of experi-ence; psychoanalytic theories emphasize unconscious urges; learning theories emphasize observable behavior; and humanistic theories emphasize the individuality and potential of each person.

3. Which theories emphasize the impact of early experience on development?

   Psychoanalytic and learning theories suggest that early experiences, such as family influences, have long-term effects, but only learning theories suggest ways to reverse those effects; cognitive and humanistic theories recognize early experiences but concentrate on current and future development.

4. How does each theory view the child?

   Each theory views the child differently: psychoanalytic theories regard the child as a collection of hidden impulses; learning theories, as a "tabula rasa" to be molded by the environment; humanistic theories, as an individual with rights, striving to fulfill his or her potential; cognitive theories, as a thinking, rational creature.

5. Do the theories use the same methodology? What is the relationship of the scientific method to the various theories?

   Each theory prefers a different methodology: learning theories, the experi-ment; cognitive theories, the clinical interview method; psychoanalytic theories, the case study with psychiatric clients among the subjects; humanis-tic theories, the case study of normal, healthy persons.

   All four theories emphasize careful observation in combination with theoret-ical principles; however, only the learning and cognitive theorists have made extensive efforts to test their principles through the use of the scientific method.

6. How do the theories view adult development?

   The theories hold different opinions on adult development: humanistic theories hold great hope for the continuing growth of adult personality; cog-nitive theories generally do not consider cognitive advances after the age of sixteen to be very interesting or important; learning theories see a constant learning process throughout the life span, with adults obeying the same laws of behavior as children; psychoanalytic theorists are split—Freud's psychosexual theory "stops" personality development at age six, while Erikson's psychosocial theory stresses the continuation of personality development throughout the life span.

AUDIO TESTBANK

Note: A testbank for the text is published separately by Worth Publishers, Inc.

Multiple Choice Questions

The correct answer to each question is identified by a capital letter.

1. According to Freud's theory, development occurs in:
   a. psychosocial stages.
   B. psychosexual stages.
   c. a continuous sequence, rather than in stages.
   d. completely unpredictable ways.

2. According to Erikson's theory, development occurs in:
   A. psychosocial stages.
   b. psychosexual stages.
   c. a continuous sequence, rather than in stages.
   d. completely unpredictable ways.

3. In contrast to Freud's theory, Erikson's theory emphasizes:
   a. unconscious urges.
   b. the importance of early experiences to the formation of personality.
   C. social and cultural influences on development.
   d. all of the above.

4. Which psychosocial stage occurs at the same time as the oral psychosexual stage?
   A. trust vs. mistrust
   b. autonomy vs. shame and doubt
   c. initiative vs. guilt
   d. industry vs. inferiority

5. According to Erikson, children who experience more shame than autonomy:
   a. will be unlikely to trust other people.
   b. may become unusually aggressive.
   c. may develop an unusually strong need for approval.
   D. may feel inferior throughout their lives.

6. According to Freud's theory, during the second and third years of life children are in the:
   a. oral stage.
   B. anal stage.

    c. phallic stage.

    d. latency stage.

7. Freud believed that personality was well established by age:

    a. 3.

    b. 5.

    C. 6.

    d. 9.

8. According to Erikson, a 4-year-old girl who is beginning to envisage goals and to think about being grown up is in the stage of:

    a. trust vs. mistrust.

    B. initiative vs. guilt.

    c. industry vs. inferiority.

    d. integrity vs. despair.

9. Freud's final stage of development, the _____ stage, begins during _____ and lasts throughout the remainder of life.

    a. latency; late childhood

    b. phallic; adolescence

    C. genital; adolescence

    d. phallic; early adulthood

10. According to Erikson, most individuals experience the crisis of identity vs. role confusion during:

    A. adolescence.

    b. early adulthood.

    c. middle adulthood.

    d. late adulthood.

11. For which of the following reasons has Erikson's theory been criticized?

    a. The theory is biased toward male development.

    b. The theory has never been tested scientifically.

    c. The theory's basic outline of life as a staircase consisting of fixed stages is inaccurate.

    D. The theory has been criticized for all of these reasons.

12. In contrast to Freud's theory, Erikson's theory emphasizes that human development is:

    A. life long.

    b. largely a matter of fate.

    c. under each individual's control.

    d. diverse, rather than stereotyped from person to person.

13. According to Freud, sexual needs become quiet during the _____ period. For Erikson, this period is a critical time of conflict between:

    a. genital; identity and role confusion.

    b. genital; industry and inferiority.

    c. latency; identity and role confusion.

    D. latency; industry and inferiority.

14. "Generativity" refers to:

    a. a desire to feel productive in one's work.

    b. the urge to be creative.

    c. the need to have children.

    D. a concern for establishing and guiding the next generation.

15. Nearing death, 83-year-old Edna feels that she has led a good and meaningful life. According to Erikson, Edna has attained a sense of:

    a. generativity.

    B. integrity.

    c. equanimity.

    d. acceptance.

Essay Questions

1. Outline Freud's five stages of psychosexual development. (audio program)

2. Outline Erikson's eight stages of psychosocial development. Explain how his theory diverges from that of Freud, and discuss its significance in life-span psychology. (audio program)

3. Describe Freud's three components of personality. Cite several contributions psychoanalytic theory has made to the study of development, and several criticisms of it. (textbook)

4. Cite several contributions learning theory has made to the study of development, and several criticisms of it. (textbook)

5. Contrast the theories of Maslow and Rogers with those emphasizing psychoanalysis and behaviorism, and cite several contributions and criticisms of humanistic theory. (textbook)

6. Outline Piaget's four stages of cognitive development and his theory of the processes by which mental growth and adaptation occur. (textbook)

7. Compare and contrast the four major theories of development and explain the eclectic perspective. (textbook)

8. Elizabeth, a 5-year-old nursery school student, is very disruptive in the classroom. Whenever she doesn't get her way she is aggressive or throws a tantrum. How might a learning theorist, cognitive psychologist, humanistic psychologist, and psychoanalytic psychologist approach this problem? Which approach do you feel would be most successful? (textbook)

9. Identify the points of agreement and disagreement in the developmental theories of Sigmund Freud and Erik Erikson. Explain why Erikson's theory has had such a major impact on the field of developmental psychology. (audio program and textbook)

10. In attempting to remedy each of the following undesirable behaviors, tell

which of the major developmental theories would be most useful and why. (textbook)

a. Although Ted cannot recall ever falling from a height, his fear of high places is extreme.
b. All her adult life, Janet has had problems with overeating and use of alcohol.
c. Six-year-old Bobby, who appears malnourished and neglected, has trouble paying attention in school.
d. Susan always expects the worst of any new situation she finds herself in; consequently she fails to enjoy her life.

References

Erikson, Erik H. (1963). *Childhood and society* (2nd ed.) New York: Norton.

This is Erikson's landmark publication which outlines the eight stages of psychosocial development.

Genetics

AUDIO PROGRAM: And Then We Knew

OVERVIEW

Audio Program 3, "And Then We Knew," and Chapter 3 of *The Developing Person Through the Life Span, 2/e,* examine **genetics,** the science concerned with the mechanisms of biological inheritance. The program focuses on the story of Karen and Don, a young couple hoping to have children despite their concerns about physical abnormalities among children on Don's side of the family. The text and program provide background for their story through a discussion of the mechanisms of heredity, including **genes, chromosomes,** and **DNA.** The textbook emphasizes that although nearly every human quality is affected by genes, most important characteristics, such as personality, intelligence, and talent, are affected by the interaction of various genetic and environmental factors.

The program and text identify the baseline risk factor that is present in every pregnancy and discuss the most typical causes of genetic abnormalities, including a **chromosome translocation. Genetic testing** based on procedures such as **amniocentesis** and **chorionic villus sampling** can help to predict whether a couple will produce a child with a genetic problem. Through use of the new technique of **gene mapping,** researchers are attempting to pinpoint the exact positions of genes responsible for inherited disorders. The deeper understanding of the causes of genetic disorders has also given rise to the possibility of **gene replacement therapy,** in which normal genes are cultivated and introduced into the tissue of a diseased person. Although the technique is still in the experimental stage, researchers have pinpointed the abnormal genes responsible for **Huntington's disease, cystic fibrosis,** and **sickle cell anemia.**

In discussing Karen and Don's situation, geneticist Dr. Donald Rucknagel and genetic counselor Diane Baker explain that although Don does not show any of the abnormalities present in other members of his family—that is, the disorder is not manifest in his **phenotype**—he is a **carrier** of the deleterious gene in his **genotype.** Faced with this information, Karen and Don must make the difficult decision of whether or not to have children. In addition to the threat it poses to Don's self-esteem, the genetic "news" has a deep impact on Karen, and on Don's mother. As the story unfolds, the listener discovers the technological advances that have made genetic counseling possible, and the impact of this technology on a particular couple and their extended families. The program concludes with the thought that although science offers more and more answers about genetically based disorders, it has also created a body of difficult questions and choices that we, our children, and future generations must face.

LESSON GOALS

1. To explain the basic mechanisms of heredity, including the significance of chromosomes and genes.

2. To describe common causes of genetic abnormalities and several techniques of genetic testing for the presence of such disorders.

3. To discuss the process and importance of genetic counseling.

LESSON 3 EXERCISE: GENETIC LEGACIES

In this exercise a more complete description is provided of the genetic abnormality (translocation of chromosomes 3 and 15) carried by Don, the husband introduced in the audio program. Students are asked to complete a chart to delineate the four possible genetic legacies Don could contribute to any children he and Karen conceive. In addition, they are asked to describe the effects of each legacy on a child's **genotype** and **phenotype.**

Since answers are provided for this exercise, there is less of a need for feedback from you to your students. However, if a follow-up is desired, this exercise could be used to initiate further thought. For example, ask students to think about the genetic legacies they received from their own parents. For which characteristics did they manifest the parental phenotype? For which do they carry only the genotype? This would also be a good opportunity to discuss further **dominant** and **recessive** genes, as well as the mathematics of heritability.

In the audio program Professor Kotre alluded to the psychological burden that genetic technology may place on prospective parents and other family members. Encourage students to be honest as they discuss their feelings about genetics, and whether the decision to have children is complicated by advances in technology. You might pose questions such as these: Should genetic screening be required for every couple? For some couples? Who should decide who gets screened? How much governmental involvement should there be in such testing?

AUDIO TESTBANK

Note: A testbank for the text is published separately by Worth Publishers, Inc.

Multiple Choice Questions

The correct answer to each question is identified by a capital letter.

1. Phenotype refers to:
   a. a person's genetic legacy.
   B. a person's actual appearance and behavior.
   c. the dominant genes a person carries.
   d. the recessive genes a person carries.

2. The threadlike structures that contain DNA and genes are called:
    a. phenotypes.
    b. genotypes.
    c. villi.
    D. chromosomes.

3. Two people who have brown eyes have the same phenotype for eye color. Which of the following is therefore true?
    a. Because they have the same phenotype, they must also have the same genotype for eye color.
    b. Because they have the same phenotype for eye color, their genotypes must be different.
    C. Although they have the same phenotype for eye color, they may or may not have the same genotype.
    d. It is impossible to determine without more information.

4. In the audio program Don was a "carrier" of a genetic disorder, yet did not actually suffer from it. This means that he manifested the abnormality:
    A. only in his genotype.
    b. only in his phenotype.
    c. in both his genotype and phenotype.
    d. in neither his genotype nor phenotype.

5. A copy of the original genotype that we inherited from both parents can be found in:
    a. our cells only prior to birth.
    b. only our sperm or ova.
    c. certain brain cells.
    D. every normal cell in our bodies.

6. The cells of the human body each contain _____ chromosomes.
    a. 23
    b. 32
    C. 46
    d. 64

7. Down syndrome is caused by a chromosomal translocation. This condition occurs when:
    a. the individual possesses fewer chromosomes than are required.
    b. the individual possesses more chromosomes than are required.
    C. a portion of one chromosome breaks off and becomes attached to some other chromosome.
    d. the genes making up a particular chromosome are deficient in DNA.

8. The prenatal diagnostic technique in which fetal tissue is withdrawn from the placenta and analyzed is called:
    a. amniocentesis.
    b. karyotyping.

   C. chorionic villus biopsy.
   d. prenatal gene mapping.

9. The experimental technique in which normal genes are introduced into some tissue of a person with a genetic disorder is called:
   a. chorionic villus sampling.
   b. amniocentesis.
   c. gene mapping.
   D. gene replacement therapy.

10. Amniocentesis is a procedure in which:
    a. blood is drawn from the abdomen of the mother.
    b. sperm is examined microscopically for genetic defects.
    c. a blood sample is drawn directly from the fetus.
    D. fluid is drawn from the uterus of the mother.

11. In any pregnancy, there is a baseline risk of an abnormal outcome. In healthy couples this baseline risk is:
    a. less than one percent.
    B. about 2 to 3 percent.
    c. about 5 percent.
    d. 7 to 10 percent.

12. For which of the following families would genetic counseling be recommended?
    a. A young couple who have a family history of a genetic disorder and wish to have a child.
    b. A family with a six-year-old child who is diagnosed as having a genetic condition.
    c. A family in which the 37-year-old father begins to manifest signs of Huntington's disease.
    D. Genetic counseling is available and recommended for each of the above families.

13. Which of the following is a single gene disorder?
    a. hemophilia
    b. sickle cell anemia
    c. cystic fibrosis
    D. All of the above are single gene disorders.

14. Which form of genetic counseling is the most widely recognized by the public?
    a. counseling for adult-onset conditions
    b. pediatric genetic counseling
    C. prenatal diagnosis
    d. geriatric counseling

15. A person's genetic makeup is called their:
    A. genotype.
    b. phenotype.

c. biological clock.
d. gene map.

Essay Questions

1. What is the difference between a person's genotype and phenotype? (audio program)

2. What is the baseline risk factor that is present in any pregnancy? (audio program)

3. How can genetic counseling help in each of the following areas? (audio program)

   a. prenatal diagnosis
   b. pediatric genetics
   c. adult-onset conditions

4. What is the significance of each of the following techniques for treating genetic abnormalities? (audio program)

   a. chorionic villus sampling
   b. gene mapping
   c. gene replacement therapy

5. What is the difference between monozygotic and dizygotic twins? How have twins been used in developmental research? (textbook)

6. Why are most human characteristics considered to be multifactorial in nature? (textbook)

7. What are some of the causes of genetic problems? (textbook)

8. Discuss the positive and negative aspects of recent technological developments in the areas of prenatal genetic diagnosis, gene mapping, and gene replacement therapy. (audio program and textbook)

9. Do you consider that genetic testing should be compulsory for every couple? Why or why not? Who should receive genetic counseling? (audio program and textbook)

10. Imagine that you are an adopted child and know nothing about your biological parents. From your phenotype, what, if anything, could you determine about them? Explain your reasoning. (textbook)

References

Plomin, R., DeFries, J.C., & McClearn, G. E. (1980). *Behavioral genetics: A primer*. San Francisco: Freeman.

Text is a helpful, readable introduction to basic genetics and genetic research.

Kessler, Seymour (ed.) (1979). *Genetic counseling: Psychological dimensions*. New York: Academic Press.

A prominent genetic counselor discusses several aspects of genetic counseling, including its philosophy and impact on the individual and society. Using numerous examples from actual case studies, Kessler emphasizes the psychological impact of genetic testing on prospective parents.

Prenatal Development and Birth

OVERVIEW

Lesson 4 of *Seasons of Life* explores issues regarding prenatal development and birth. As Kathleen Berger discusses in *The Developing Person Through the Life Span, 2/e,* the birth of a child is one of life's most enriching experiences. Nine months of prenatal development culminate in the expectant couple assuming a new and demanding role as parents and being transformed from a couple to a family. Berger describes normal prenatal development as well as some of the problems that can occur, including **preterm birth,** low birth weight, and prenatal exposure to disease, drugs, environmental hazards, and other **teratogens.** Also discussed in this chapter is the growing awareness in our society that the birth experience of babies and their parents is influenced by many factors, including the preparation provided by childbirth classes, the active participation of both mother and father in the birth, and the tendency of our culture toward the **medicalization** of birth.

In audio program 4, "When to Have a Baby," two couples about to give birth to their first child discuss their impending parenthood. Because one of the expectant mothers is 21 and the other 36, the life-span consequences of their "early" and "late" births will be very different. Their stories, illuminated by the expert commentary of sociologist Alice Rossi and anthropologist Jane Lancaster, illustrate how the three **developmental clocks** introduced in Lesson 1 influence the timing of births. As becomes apparent, whether 21 is too young to become a parent or 36 is too old is an individual matter determined by the settings of these three clocks. The timing of these births focuses the listener's awareness on a major theme of the series: that the diversity of development through the life span is partly due to the fact that the social and psychological clocks are not the same for everyone. Just as each culture, subculture, and historical period establishes its own social clock, so each individual establishes a psychological clock on the basis of his or her particular life experiences.

As the program opens we hear the two couples pondering one of life's major transitions: from being an expectant couple to being parents.

LESSON GOALS

1. To differentiate the biological clock, the social clock, and the psychological clock, and discuss their significance in the timing of births.

2. To discuss how the timing of births and the setting of the three developmental clocks have changed over the course of human history.

3. To outline the rapid and orderly development that occurs between conception and birth.

4. To explain the general risk factors and specific hazards that may affect prenatal development.

5. To discuss the psychological impact of pregnancy and birth on expectant parents.

LESSON 4 EXERCISE: SAYING WHEN

Throughout the *Seasons of Life* series the effects of the biological, social, and psychological clocks on each person's life are emphasized. In several of the lessons the exercise requires students to consider the settings of these clocks in their own lives. The exercise for Lesson 4 asks them to do so regarding the timing of births. The settings of the developmental clocks can affect the timing of births, the adjustment of first-time parents to their new roles, and can have long-term life-span consequences on both children and parents.

The stories of the two couples introduced in Audio Program 4 illustrate two patterns of childbearing. Shelley McKean and her husband Charles gave birth when Shelley was 21. Shelley's pregnancy was "on time" biologically, but "off time" socially and psychologically. The pregnancy was unexpected and came at a time when the young couple was still establishing their own relationship, completing their educations, and struggling to make a living.

Brett and Henry's child was born when Brett was 36. This biologically "late" birth is an example of an increasingly common pattern of childbearing that favors the social clock by allowing parents to establish careers and improve their financial security before having children. Brett and Henry's birth may have been "off time" biologically, but it was "on time" psychologically and "on time," or perhaps even a little late, in terms of the social clock.

To help students integrate the material in Lesson 4 into their own lives, they are asked to write answers to several questions regarding the timing of births of their own children, or children they may have in the future.

Since there are no correct or incorrect answers for this exercise, the most appropriate feedback might be a summary of the class's answers. The summary need not be exhaustive, but should note any cohort effects in the timing of births. Regarding the actual (or anticipated) timing of their children's births, are there generational differences in the settings of your students' developmental clocks? Is there a trend in recent years toward the two new patterns of child-bearing outlined in the program? If your students' data are consistent with this trend, this feedback would be a particularly effective validation of the program's content.

AUDIO TESTBANK

Note: A testbank for the text is published separately by Worth Publishers, Inc.

Multiple Choice Questions

The correct answer to each question is identified by a capital letter.

1. The biological clock refers to:
    a. society's age norms for when certain life events should happen.
    B. the body's mechanisms governing physical development.
    c. each person's inner timetable for their own development.
    d. the biological and environmental forces that govern longevity.

2. For women, the optimal period of fertility is between the ages of _____;
    for men optimal fertility occurs between the ages of _____
    A. 22 and 32 . . . 22 and 40.
    b. 20 and 40 . . . 18 and 45.
    c. 18 and 30 . . . 18 and 35.
    d. 16 and 30 . . . 16 and 35.

3. According to the audio program, biologically early births may be associated
    with _____; late births are associated with increased risk of disorders such
    as _____
    a. bonding failure; microencephaly.
    b. preterm delivery; Klinefelter's syndrome.
    C. low birth weight babies; Down syndrome.
    d. uterine cancer; mongolism.

4. The social clock represents:
    A. society's age norms for when certain life events should happen.
    b. the body's mechanisms governing physical development.
    c. each person's inner timetable for their own development.
    d. the biological and environmental forces that govern longevity.

5. Unlike the biological clock, the social clock:
    a. does not usually change significantly from generation to generation.
    b. is the same for people throughout the world.
    c. is different in women and men.
    D. can be reset from generation to generation.

6. Since World War II, the average age at which women and men married:
    a. has increased steadily with each passing year.
    b. has decreased steadily with each passing year.
    C. first decreased and then, in the last twenty years, increased.
    d. has not changed significantly.

7. The psychological clock refers to:
    a. society's age norms for when certain life events should happen.

    b. the body's mechanisms governing physical development.

    C. each person's inner timetable for his or her own development.

    d. the biological and environmental forces that govern longevity.

8. For most of our species' history:

    a. humans existed as hunter–gatherers.

    b. humans lived a nomadic existence.

    c. humans lived in small groups of nuclear families.

    D. all of the above statements were true.

9. The term "sedentism" refers to:

    a. the wandering lifestyle of early humans.

    B. the village-dwelling lifestyle that humans adopted when agriculture was invented.

    c. the suppression of ovulation that tends to accompany continuous nursing.

    d. the tendency of modern women and men to postpone childbearing.

10. The term "menarche" refers to:

    A. the first menstrual period.

    b. the first ovulation of a fertile egg.

    c. the age at which sexual interest begins.

    d. the first year of menstruation.

11. In the course of our species' history, the change to a sedentary lifestyle was associated with:

    A. more frequent production of children.

    b. less frequent production of children.

    c. an increase in the average age of menarche.

    d. a decrease in the average age of menarche.

12. For what reasons, according to the audio program, are the biological and social clocks "out of sync" for today's maturing adults?

    A. Although reproductive maturity today occurs at an earlier age than in the past, it takes longer to achieve the status of an adult.

    b. Because of society's pressure to rush development, children today assume many responsibilities of an adult before they have attained reproductive maturity.

    c. Most adults today have their first child outside the range of optimal fertility.

    d. Better nutrition and health care have so lengthened the years of fertility that social role has largely become irrelevant in the timing of births.

13. Today, the typical American mother:

    a. experiences approximately nine times the number of menstrual cycles that her ancestors did.

    b. gives birth to two children, a few years apart.

    c. has two new patterns of childbearing: one favoring the social clock and one favoring the biological clock.

    D. shows all of the above characteristics.

14. Research reported in the audio program has shown that only children:

    a. tend to be more spoiled and egocentric.

    B. may be more adult-oriented.

    c. are often lonesome.

    d. show none of the characteristics listed above.

15. According to the audio program, what is one outcome of the increasing tendency of couples to time childbearing so as to favor the social clock?

    a. Family size is increasing as parents begin their childbearing at a younger age.

    B. The one-child family is becoming more common as parents begin their childbearing later.

    c. Birth-order effects are becoming more pronounced as parents are spacing their children over longer periods.

    d. Birth-order effects are becoming less pronounced as parents are spacing their children closer together.

Essay Questions

1. Differentiate the biological clock, the social clock, and the psychological clock and discuss their significance in development through the life span. (audio program)

2. Discuss whether the settings of the three developmental clocks are different for different generations. (audio program)

3. Explain how the pattern and timing of childbearing changed as humans shifted from a hunting-and-gathering society to a modern society. (audio program)

4. Discuss some of the life-span consequences of births that occur early and late in parents' lives. (audio program)

5. Describe the significant developments that occur in each of the three periods of prenatal development: the germinal period, the period of the embryo, and the period of the fetus. (textbook)

6. Identify several psychological factors that influence parents' overall experience of birth and describe several approaches to improving this experience. (textbook)

7. Discuss whether there is a critical period in development for the formation of the parent–infant bond. (textbook)

8. Discuss some of the positive and negative aspects of the two new trends in the timing of childbearing. (audio program and textbook)

9. In the audio program, you learned about some of the factors that have resulted in the biological and social clocks becoming "out of sync." What

are some of these factors and what do you foresee as their influence on the timing of childbearing in future generations? (audio program)

10. Imagine that your newlywed daughter and son-in-law are contemplating having children. What advice would you offer regarding the best time to have a baby? (audio program and textbook)

References

Kitzinger, Sheila (1985). *Birth over thirty.* New York: Penguin.

Kitzinger examines various aspects of pregnancies in older women, including physical risks such as Down syndrome and cesarean births as well as psychological aspects, such as how to adjust to the role of motherhood during middle age.

The First Two Years: Physical Development

AUDIO PROGRAM: The Biography of the Brain

OVERVIEW

This is the first of a three-lesson unit that describes the developing person from birth to age 2 in terms of physical, cognitive, and psychosocial development. Lesson 5 examines physical development.

In Chapter 5 of the textbook, Kathleen Berger describes the typical patterns of growth in the body and nervous system along with the timetables of sensory, perceptual, and motor-skill development. Variations in the ages at which certain skills are mastered are attributed to the interaction of biological and environmental forces.

Audio Program 5, "The Biography of the Brain," continues the stories of the two couples introduced in Program 4. Both couples have now had their babies, and in this lesson we follow the early months of their infants' physical development. Evolutionary biologist Stephen Jay Gould and anthropologist Barry Bogin point out how immature humans are at birth. Were our babies more developed, these experts suggest, their heads would not fit through the birth canal.

The importance of good nutrition and a stimulating environment to the developing brain are also discussed in Program 5. Expert commentary is provided by anthropologist Jane Lancaster and neuropsychologist Jill Becker. Brain development is described at the microscopic level as a process in which individual neurons grow and form synapses with other neurons.

As the program unfolds, the listener discovers the pacing of physical development over the entire life span reflects the pre-eminent role of the human brain.

LESSON GOALS

1. To describe the normal patterns of physical, brain, and motor skill development during infancy.

2. To discuss how biological environmental forces interact in sensory development, brain maturation, and the acquisition of motor skills.

3. To identify the competing evolutionary pressures that have led some anthropologists to argue that human babies are born "too soon."

4. To outline the nutritional needs of infants during the first year of life and describe the significance of breast milk and body fat in ensuring adequate nutrition.

LESSON 5 EXERCISE: GROWTH RATES AND MOTOR SKILL DEVELOPMENT IN THE FIRST 2 YEARS

The student exercise for Lesson 5 concerns physical growth and motor skill development during infancy. By projecting the typical growth patterns of infants onto their own bodies or those of another adult, students will gain an especially vivid appreciation of the phenomenal rate of growth that occurs during this season. Students are asked to complete the following questions. Computational procedures and correct answers are provided following each question.

1. Most newborns seem top-heavy because their heads are equivalent to about one-fourth of their total length, compared to one-fifth at a year and one-eighth in adulthood. Their legs, in turn, represent only about one-fourth of total body length, whereas an adult's legs account for about one-half. Based on your present height in inches, what would be the lengths of your head and legs if they remained in the same proportions as when you were born?

   Example: For a person 5 ft. 10 in. tall, the "infant proportions" would equate to length of 17.5 inches ($\frac{1}{4} \times 70$ in.) for both head and legs, as compared to a normal adult head size of 8.75 inches ($\frac{1}{8} \times 70$ in.) and leg length of 35 inches ($\frac{1}{2} \times 70$ in.)

2. If you were gaining weight at the rate of an infant, your weight would be tripled one year from today. Calculate how much you would weigh.

   Example: Based on this rate of weight gain, a person who currently weighs 125 pounds would weigh 375 pounds (3×125) at the end of one year.

3. If you, like an infant, grew an inch a month, this would not mark such a significant growth rate—since you are much taller than an infant to begin with. Thus, every inch is a smaller percentage increase for you. Nevertheless, assume that you will grow at the rate of an infant in the first year, adding an inch a month. What would your height be a year from today?

   Example: Based on this rate of growth, one foot in height is gained each year. Thus, a person currently 5 ft. 8 inches tall would be 6 ft. 8 inches at the end of one year.

4. The same kind of calculations can help you make a less dramatic comparison between growth rates in the first and second years of life. In the first year, weight triples; thus an infant born at a little more than 7 pounds will weigh about 21 pounds at one year. If growth were to continue at this rate, how much would the child weigh at two years? (In fact, the average infant at two years weights only 30 pounds).

   Example: A child who weighs 21 pounds at one year would weigh 63 pounds (3×21) at the end of the year.

5. The average infant grows an inch a month in the first year. If a 30-inch one-year-old continued growing at this rate, how tall would he or she be at two years? (In fact, the faster growing child grows only 6 inches, to reach 36 inches at age two.)

Answer: A 30-inch one-year-old gaining an inch in height per month would be 42 inches tall (30 + 12) at the end of the second year.

6. Pick up a piece of paper or some other small object with your whole hand, that is, with all fingers curled around it. What kind of grasp is this?

   Answer: ulnar grasp

7. Now hold the paper between your middle fingers and the palm of your hand. What kind of grasp is this?

   Answer: palmar grasp

8. Pick up the paper with your index finger pressed against the side of your palm. Name this kind of grasp.

   Answer: radial grasp

9. Finally, use the thumb and index finger to pick up the paper. What is the name of this grasp, and when is it achieved?

   Answer: pincer grasp, sometime between 9 and 14 months.

10. Which of these ways of grasping a small object felt most comfortable or natural to you?

Since this exercise is self-explanatory, a follow-up from the instructor is not essential. The instructor may wish to check the accuracy of students' answers, however, and return corrected exercise sheets.

AUDIO TESTBANK

Note: A testbank for the text is published separately by Worth Publishers, Inc.

Multiple Choice Questions

The correct answer to each question is identified by a capital letter.

1. For what reason(s) do some anthropologists believe that human gestation has been accelerated over evolutionary time?
   a. Since very little human behavior is innate, prenatal development time is relatively short.
   B. If prenatal development continued any longer the human's large brain and head would make vaginal birth impossible.
   c. The helpless state of the human newborn promotes stronger parent-child attachment.
   d. for all of the above reasons

2. How do newborn human infants compare to other primates in terms of body composition?
   A. They have more body fat.
   b. They have less body fat.
   c. They have about the same amount of body fat.
   d. They are more muscular.

3. Most of the development of the human brain occurs:
    a. during the first 3 months of the pregnancy.
    b. during the middle 3 months of the pregnancy.
    c. during the last 3 months of the pregnancy.
    D. following birth.

4. According to experts on the program, what is one of the main reasons mothers store body fat during their pregnancies and afterwards?
    a. To insulate the developing embryo from environmental hazards.
    b. Because the mother's metabolism slows during her pregnancy and calories are more readily converted to fat.
    C. To ensure an adequate supply of nutrients for milk production.
    d. for all of the above reasons

5. Compared to the milk of most other species, human milk:
    a. has about twice the protein.
    b. has about three times as much protein.
    c. is higher in fat.
    D. is higher in sugar.

6. The nerve cells of the brain are called:
    A. neurons.
    b. synapses.
    c. endocrines.
    d. interneurons.

7. All of the nerve cells a human brain will ever possess are first present:
    a. at conception.
    b. about 3 months following conception.
    C. at birth.
    d. at age 5 or 6, when the child begins school.

8. Connections in the brain where nerve cells communicate with one another are called:
    a. neurons.
    B. synapses.
    c. endocrines.
    d. interneurons.

9. One effect on the developing brain of exposure to a stimulating environment is:
    a. the formation of fewer synapses.
    b. a reduction in the number of surplus nerve cells that survive.
    C. the development of more branches and neural connections on surviving brain cells.
    d. all of the above.

10. The average number of synapses in the brain of a 2-year-old:
    a. is about the same as that in the brain of an adult.
    b. is slightly less than that in the brain of an adult.

    c. is much less than that in the brain of an adult.

    D. is much greater than that in the brain of an adult.

11. Which of the following is true concerning how the brain responds to environmental stimulation?

    a. Synapses are made and broken throughout life.

    b. Even in old age nerve cells will respond to stimulation by growing extra branches.

    c. Neural insulation continues to form during early adulthood.

    D. All of the above are true.

12. Which of the following most accurately describes the growth curve for the human body?

    A. From birth to 2 the growth curve is very steep, leveling off to a steady rate until puberty, when it is again steep.

    b. From birth until puberty the growth curve is fairly flat, reflecting a steady rate until the adolescent growth spurt.

    c. The curve is steep during infancy and flat over the remainder of the life span.

    d. The curve peaks during infancy and falls over the remainder of the life span.

13. Which of the following is the correct order in which the body, the brain, and the reproductive system mature in humans?

    a. reproductive system, body, brain

    b. body, reproductive system, brain

    c. body, brain, reproductive system

    D. brain, body, reproductive system

14. What explanation is offered in the program for the sequence of physical development in humans?

    a. Nerve cells divide more rapidly than cells that comprise other body tissues.

    b. The body's final growth spurt can only occur following the hormonal surge that is triggered by sexual maturity.

    C. Body growth and sexual maturity are delayed until the brain reaches its full capacity.

    d. Hormonal production, which governs development of the reproductive system, depends on the body having attained its full growth.

15. According to experts in the program, two competing evolutionary pressures on the shape of the hips in humans have been:

    a. having fewer children and increased longevity.

    B. the advantages of walking upright and having a large brain at birth.

    c. reduced body fat and increased muscle mass.

    d. the advantages of sedentary living and an agricultural existence.

Essay Questions

1. Explain why some anthropologists believe that, compared with other mammals, human babies are very immature at birth. (audio program)

2. Discuss the significance of breast milk and body fat in meeting the nutritional needs of the newborn. (audio program)

3. Describe the ways in which the nervous system matures during childhood. (audio program)

4. Describe the size and proportions of the average newborn's body, how these change during infancy, and how they compare to those of an average adult. (textbook)

5. Describe the sensory and perceptual abilities of the human infant. (textbook)

6. Outline the basic pattern of motor skill development in humans. (textbook)

7. Discuss the causes and results of malnutrition among children in developing countries and the United States. (textbook)

8. Tell how human development, from conception until adulthood, reflects the needs of the developing brain. (audio program)

9. Bill and Karen are concerned that their one-year-old daughter is not mastering motor skills as rapidly as their neighbor's infant. What advice would you offer these concerned parents? (textbook)

10. Imagine that in the evolutionary history of our species an upright and bi-pedal (two-footed) posture did not evolve. How might human development over the life span be different today as a result? (audio program and textbook)

References

Bogin, B. (1988) *Patterns of growth.* Cambridge, England: Cambridge University Press.

Professor Bogin, who is heard on the audio program, presents a cross-cultural perspective on physical growth and discusses longitudinal studies of the effects of chronic malnourishment in early childhood on physical and intellectual development.

The First Two Years: Cognitive Development

AUDIO PROGRAM: First Words

OVERVIEW

Lesson 6 of *Seasons of Life* considers **cognitive development**—the ways in which individuals learn about, think about, and adapt to their surroundings—during the first two years. During this short span of time infants are transformed from babies who can only know their world through a small set of reflexes into toddlers capable of imitating others, anticipating and remembering events, and pretending. Most significant is the development of language. By the end of this season of life the average toddler has a relatively large vocabulary (about 500 words) and is able to converse effectively with others.

Chapter 6 of *The Developing Person Through the Life Span, 2/e,* begins by describing and evaluating Piaget's first six stages of **sensorimotor development.** Although many psychologists believe that Piaget overemphasized motor skills and that development is more continuous than his stages imply, most accept his general outline of cognitive growth as an accurate description of developmental *functions,* if not of individual differences.

After a discussion of the "American Question"—the problems and advantages of attempting to accelerate children's cognitive development—the chapter contrasts the theories of language development proposed by Skinner and by Chomsky and describes the acquisition of language during the first two years.

Audio program 6, "First Words," provides an in-depth analysis of language acquisition from the first cry until the first word is spoken. Psycholinguist Jill deVilliers discusses several issues, including the difficulties of studying language acquisition in young children, the universal aspects of language development, the **baby talk** of parents, and the criteria used to determine when a vocalization represents the first actual word. During the program, the major landmarks of language development during infancy—**crying, cooing,** and **babbling**—are illustrated with examples of children's speech in English, Spanish, and Japanese.

An important theme of this lesson is the interaction between maturation and learning in cognitive development. This issue is discussed in the context of Piaget's theory and again in the consideration of language acquisition. Most developmental psychologists view the development of language, and cognitive functions in general, as an interactional process that reflects both nature and nurture.

LESSON GOALS

1. To outline and evaluate the theory of sensorimotor development proposed by Piaget.

2. To explain and contrast the theories of language development proposed by B. F. Skinner and Noam Chomsky.

3. To describe language development during the first two years.

LESSON 6 EXERCISE: BABY TALK

Both the audio program and textbook discuss **baby talk,** the special form of language used by adults when talking to infants. The function of baby talk is to facilitate early language acquisition. Baby talk differs from adult speech in several ways: it is distinct in pitch (higher), intonation (more exaggerated and more low-to-high fluctuations), vocabulary (simpler and more concrete), and sentence length (shorter). Baby talk is also more repetitive and uses more questions, fewer utterances involving the past tense, fewer pronouns, and fewer complex sentences. It uses **scaffolding** to support and foster conversation in children.

The exercise for Lesson 6 asks students to make arrangements to listen to an adult having a ten- to fifteen-minute conversation with an infant or toddler. Afterwards, students are to answer several questions, and return their answers to the instructor.

As a follow-up to this exercise, the instructor could prepare a summary of students' responses, particularly those to questions (3) and (4) regarding adult baby talk. In addition, the instructor could provide feedback regarding the accuracy of each student's assessment of the child's stage of language development (question 5). Alternatively, the instructor could ask students to write several paragraphs discussing the importance of baby talk in promoting language development. Students might also be asked to predict whether B. F. Skinner and Noam Chomsky would be likely to agree, or to disagree, regarding the significance of baby talk. The language issue could also be integrated with the textbook's discussion of Piaget and the "American Question" by asking students to predict how Piaget might have regarded the significance of baby talk and scaffolding in promoting cognitive development.

AUDIO TESTBANK

Note: A testbank for the text is published separately by Worth Publishers, Inc.

Multiple Choice Questions

The correct answer to each question is identified by a capital letter.

1. Cognitive development is best described as:
   A. the ways in which our thought processes evolve over our life times.
   b. the process by which children become socialized by their culture.
   c. the biological maturation of brain regions that underlie memory and thinking.
   d. all of the above.

2. The very first methods used by linguists to study language development:

    a. were based on tape recordings of children's speech.
    B. involved diaries of the vocalizations of their children.
    c. were based on computer models developed by cognitive psychologists.
    d. resulted in the proliferation of myths regarding how language is acquired.

3. Most infants begin babbling at about:

    a. 2 months
    b. 4 months
    C. 6 months
    d. 8 months

4. A literal translation of the word "infant" is:

    a. "one who crawls."
    b. "without intelligence."
    c. "smiling one."
    D. "not speaking."

5. The earliest rudiments of language are found in:

    a. cooing.
    b. babbling.
    C. crying.
    d. one-word speech.

6. Which is the correct sequence of stages of language acquisition?

    a. crying, babbling, cooing, first word
    B. crying, cooing, babbling, first word
    c. crying, babbling, first word, cooing
    d. crying, cooing, first word, babbling

7. Cooing generally begins between the ages of:

    a. one and two months.
    B. two and four months.
    c. four and six months.
    d. six and ten months.

8. The child who utters, "da, da, da, da, da" is most likely in the stage of:

    a. crying.
    b. cooing.
    C. babbling.
    d. scaffolding.

9. Compared to cooing, which has a more _____ function, babbling represents the infant's _____ with the sounds of language.

    a. cognitive . . . experimentation
    b. biological . . . frustration
    c. cognitive . . . frustration
    D. social . . . experimentation

10. On the average, at what age do children begin speaking actual words?
    a. 6 months
    b. 8 months
    c. 10 months
    D. 1 year

11. Which of the following words would a child be most likely to say first?
    a. diaper
    b. mad
    C. dog
    d. crib

12. Compared to hearing babies, deaf babies:
    a. babble at about the same age.
    b. coo at about the same age.
    c. make the same crying, cooing, and babbling sounds.
    D. do all of the above.

13. The distinct form of language called "baby talk" refers to the:
    A. simplified language that adults use when talking to young children.
    b. pre-word "speech" of infants.
    c. low-pitched sounds that babies use in the presence of their mothers.
    d. type of speech that mothers, but not fathers or nonparents, use with children.

14. Which of the following is an example of "scaffolding?"
    a. Nine-month-old Kelly refers to any four-legged animal she sees as "doggy," any woman as "Mommy," and any man as "Daddy."
    b. In talking with her four-month-old daughter, Jeanne speaks in a low-pitched voice, using very simple phrases, and speaking only about events in the past.
    C. In reading a new story to his one-year-old son, Brad reads very slowly and with exaggerated intonation. The second time he reads the story he pauses at certain points and waits for his son to make some of the noises of the animals in the story.
    d. All of the above are examples of scaffolding.

15. A listener hearing a recording of Japanese, Spanish, and North American children babbling would:
    a. not be able to tell them apart.
    b. be able to tell them apart if they were older than 6 months.
    C. be able to tell them apart if they were older than 8–10 months.
    d. be able to tell them apart at any age after the stage of cooing.

Essay Questions

1. Outline the basic sequence and landmarks of language development from birth until the first word is spoken. (audio program)

2. Identify the characteristics of baby talk, the special form of language that adults use to talk to children. (audio program)

3. Explain how parents use "scaffolding" to encourage conversation in their children. (audio program)

4. Describe the components of the six stages of sensorimotor development according to Piaget. (textbook)

5. Outline the basic sequence and landmarks of language development from the time the first word is spoken until the end of the second year. (textbook)

6. Cite several criticisms of Piaget's theory of infant cognitive development. (textbook)

7. Explain the disagreement between Piaget and many North American psychologists regarding the value of providing enriched learning programs for infants. (textbook)

8. What reasons can you offer to explain the fact that baby talk seems to have similar characteristics throughout the world? (audio program and textbook)

9. Imagine that you have been asked to babysit for your 8-month-old cousin. What kinds of activities should you plan for the baby? Explain your reasoning. (textbook)

10. Contrast the theories of language acquisition of Skinner and Chomsky and tell which theory seems most correct to you, giving your reasons for feeling as you do. (textbook)

References

deVilliers, Jill G. and deVilliers, Peter A. (1978). *Language acquisition.* Cambridge, MA: Harvard University Press.

This scholarly resource on language development is written by two eminent researchers, including Jill deVilliers, who is heard on the audio program.

The First Two Years: Psychosocial Development

AUDIO PROGRAM: Attachment: The Dance Begins

OVERVIEW

Lesson 7, which covers psychosocial development during the first two years, completes a three-lesson unit on development during infancy. In this lesson, the child's emerging self-awareness, personality, emotional expression, and relationship to parents and society are explored.

Chapter 7 of the textbook outlines the developmental sequence of various emotions and discusses several theories of personality development (Freud, Erikson, and Mahler) that help us understand emotional development. Kathleen Berger points out the traditional view of personality development considered the infant a passive recipient of the personality created by an "omnipotent mother." It is now apparent that many personality traits are present at birth, before parental influence is felt.

The chapter also discusses **child abuse** and **neglect,** which are explained as the product of many interrelated factors, including the parents' background, the child's behavior, the stresses of daily life, and even cultural attitudes about children.

Audio Program 7, "Attachment: The Dance Begins," explores the who, when, where, and why of **attachment** between infants and their primary care-givers. Attachment, which helps ensure infants receive the adult care required for survival, emerges in infants the world over at about 6 or 7 months. This is when babies begin to realize people don't cease to exist when they're out of sight. Several important issues regarding attachment are discussed, including the impact of adoption, day care, and insecure attachment on the developing child. Expert commentary is provided by psychologists Michael Lamb, Janice Gibson, and Sheldon White.

An important theme of this lesson is that attachment, an intricate "dance" between infant and care-giver, lays the foundation for psychosocial development throughout the seasons of life.

LESSON GOALS

1. To outline the development of basic emotions and personality characteristics, both in theory and as observed in fact.

2. To discuss the significance of parent-infant interaction in the infant's psycho-social development.

3. To describe the characteristics of a good home environment, a poor home environment, and an abusive one.

4. To discuss issues related to attachment, including its timing, participants, and long-term impact on psychosocial development.

LESSON 7 EXERCISE: ATTACHMENT AND THE "STRANGE SITUATION"

The exercise for Lesson 7 is designed to increase students' understanding of how attachment is measured. Students are to arrange to observe a one- or two-year-old child and his or her care-giver in a play setting outside of the child's home. During the observation period, the infant's reactions to a novel situation and the comings and goings of its care-giver are measured.

Most infants demonstrate secure attachment in this situation. The presence of their mother gives them the sense of security needed to express their natural curiosity and explore the test room. If their mother makes a move to leave the room, securely attached infants will usually stop playing, verbally protest, and demonstrate contact-seeking behaviors, such as crying and calling.

Approximately one-third of infants show insecure attachment in this test situation, clinging nervously to their mother and being unwilling to explore even while she remains in the room.

After the ten- to fifteen-minute observation period, students are to complete several questions and return these answers to their instructor.

The instructor might check the descriptions of the behavior of child and parent during the observation and determine whether the designation of the child as securely attached or insecurely attached seems appropriate. If not, a natural follow-up to this exercise would be to ask the students to substantiate their answers. An alternative follow-up would be to ask students some of the following questions: Do you feel that the strange situation is a valid test of secure attachment? Why or why not? In what other ways could parent-child attachment be measured? What advice would you offer to the parents of an insecurely attached child? To expectant parents hoping to foster secure attachment in their child?

AUDIO TESTBANK

Note: A testbank for the text is published separately by Worth Publishers, Inc.

Multiple Choice Questions

The correct answer to each question is identified by a capital letter.

1. The specific tie that develops between an infant and its primary care-giver is called:
   a. bonding.
   B. attachment.

    c. synchronization.

    d. affiliation.

2. For what reason do developmental psychologists believe that the timing of attachment is biologically based?

    a. Children who do not become securely attached show retarded physical development.

    b. Attachment derives from proximity-seeking behaviors that are triggered by hormones in the mother's body.

    C. Attachment happens with such regularity around the world that it must be biologically based.

    d. Attachment is so unpredictable that only individual biological differences could account for the variation in its timing.

3. Attachment between mothers and infants occurs when infants are approximately how old?

    a. 1 week

    b. 1 month

    c. 3 months

    D. 6-7 months

4. The timing of attachment has been attributed to the baby's new ability to:

    A. cognitively represent other individuals.

    b. visually focus on a moving object.

    c. anticipate future events.

    d. hold its head upright.

5. Which of the following is true concerning the role of early contact between mothers and infants?

    a. Mothers denied early contact with their infants do not develop strong attachment.

    b. Most abusive mothers were prevented from having early contact with their babies.

    C. There is no good evidence that early contact has a major impact on the quality of attachment.

    d. Both a and b are true.

6. Babies give their first real smiles, called _____, when they are about _____ of age.

    a. play smiles; 3 months

    b. play smiles; 4 to 6 weeks

    c. social smiles; 3 months

    D. social smiles; 4 to 6 weeks

7. Concerning the placement of children with adoptive parents, which of the following is true?

    a. It is easier to place a child in an adoptive home before it reaches 6 months of age, when it forms its first attachment.

    b. Children placed with adoptive parents after 6 or 7 months of age may first have to go through a process of grieving the loss of an earlier attachment.

    c. Babies are generally resilient and can recover from the breaking of one attachment or wait for the forming of their first attachment.

    D. All of the above are true.

8. Which of the following is a clear sign of a baby's attachment to a particular person?

    a. The baby turns to that person when distressed.

    b. The baby protests when that person leaves.

    c. The baby may cry when strangers appear.

    D. All of the above are signs of attachment.

9. Concerning the impact of day care on attachment, which of the following is true?

    a. There is a significant increase in the likelihood that babies in day care will be insecurely attached to their mothers.

    b. Psychologists believe that one unavoidable negative impact of day care is that babies often form multiple attachments.

    C. Approximately two-thirds of babies form secure attachments to their mothers, regardless of whether or not they are placed in day care.

    d. Babies placed in day care usually become more securely attached to their mothers than babies not placed in day care.

10. A transitional object is a(n):

    A. stuffed animal, favorite blanket, or other object that children keep near them when apart from their primary care-givers.

    b. sign that a child is insecurely attached and needs more attention from his or her primary care-giver.

    c. indication that the child is ready to take the next step in becoming independent from his or her parent.

    d. all of the above.

11. In Erik Erikson's terms, becoming securely attached provides a foundation of _____ for other social behaviors in the rest of the life course.

    a. industry

    b. initiative

    C. basic trust

    d. ego identity

12. Compared to children who are insecurely attached, those who are securely attached are:

    a. more independent.

    b. more cooperative.

    c. more sociable.

    D. characterized by all of the above.

13. The later consequences of secure attachment and insecure attachment for children are:
    A. balanced by the child's current rearing circumstances.
    b. irreversible, regardless of the child's current rearing circumstances.
    c. more significant in girls than in boys.
    d. more significant in boys than in girls.

14. According to experts in the program, the formation of multiple attachments between the child and several care-givers:
    a. almost always has a permanent negative impact on the child.
    b. temporarily has a negative impact on the child, but not necessarily a long-lasting one.
    C. doesn't seem to be harmful to children.
    d. is not possible: children are capable of only one attachment at a time.

15. The most important variable in the effect that day care has on a child is:
    a. the number of hours each day the child is in the day care center.
    b. whether the child is able to spend "quality time" with his or her parents at the end of the day.
    C. the quality of day care and the extent to which day care matches the parents' style.
    d. All of the above are equally important variables in day care.

Essay Questions

1. Define attachment, outline its development, and tell why experts believe it to be a biologically determined event. (audio program)

2. Discuss the impact of early mother-infant contact, adoption, and day care on attachment. (audio program)

3. Discuss the immediate and long-range impact on infants of secure and insecure attachment. (audio program)

4. Identify and describe the developmental course of at least three emotions that are shown during the first two years of life. (textbook)

5. Identify the first two stages of personality development according to Erikson's theory and describe the healthy outcome of each. (textbook)

6. Discuss the significance of synchrony and attachment in parent-infant interaction and psychosocial development. (textbook)

7. Identify the characteristics of a child's home environment that promote psychosocial development. (textbook)

8. Erik Erikson once remarked, "Babies control and bring up families as much as they are controlled by them." What do you think he meant? Your answer should encompass development governed by each of the three developmental clocks. (audio program and textbook)

9. Describe an aspect of your personality or behavior that was strongly influenced by genetics and one that probably was learned. Provide evidence for your answer. (audio program and textbook)

10. What are some of the reasons that siblings raised by the same parents may have very different temperaments? (textbook)

References

Sroufe, L. Alan. (1978). Attachment and the roots of competence. *Human Nature.* *1*. 50-57.

Sroufe, L. Alan. (1985). Attachment classification from the perspective of infant-care-giver relationships and infant temperament. *Child Development, 56,* 1-14.

Professor Sroufe discusses the importance of attachment in psychosocial development.

The Play Years: Physical Developi

AUDIO PROGRAM: "How To" Time

OVERVIEW

Lesson 8 is the first of a three-lesson unit that describes the developing person from 2 to 6 in terms of physical, cognitive, and social development. Lesson 8 examines physical development.

During these years—often referred to as early childhood, or the preschool period—the most significant growth is the continued maturation of the nervous system and the refinement of the visual, muscular, and cognitive skills necessary for beginning school. The brain continues to develop faster than any other part of the body, attaining 90 percent of adult weight and size by the time children start school.

Children grow steadily taller, slimmer, and stronger during the active preschool years. Large body movements, such as jumping and running, improve significantly as children spend most of their waking hours at play. One of the themes of the textbook is that play is the "work" of children. For this reason Kathleen Berger refers to the preschool years as the "play years." Chapter 8 includes descriptions of **sensorimotor play, mastery play,** and **rough-and-tumble play,** and delivers the important message that it is through play that children master the motor and social skills they will need as adults.

Play is especially appropriate for the extended period of childhood that has been programmed into the biological clock. Audio Program 8, "'How To' Time," explores the evolutionary origins of childhood and the use to which we humans have put it.

The biological clock of humans delays the onset of reproduction and gives children time to acquire what Erik Erikson referred to as a sense of **industry.** Childhood is the time to pretend, to play, and to learn how to do things. And herein lies the key to our extended childhood: More than any other species, humans are dependent on complex, learned behavior for survival. The significance of "how to" time is explored through the expert commentary of pediatrician Howard Weinblatt, endocrinologist Inese Beitins, anthropologist Barry Bogin, and evolutionary biologist Stephen Jay Gould.

LESSON GOALS

1. To describe physical development during the preschool years and discuss how physical maturation is related to school readiness.

2. To outline the development of gross and fine motor skills during early childhood, and to describe those activities which foster these skills.

3. To compare and contrast physical development in preschool girls and boys.

4. To discuss the significance of the extended period of human childhood and the importance of play in development.

LESSON 8 EXERCISE: PLAY SPACES AND PLAYGROUNDS

A central theme of this lesson is that "play is the work of childhood." Developmental psychologists view play as a major means through which physical, cognitive, and social skills are mastered. Unfortunately, many adults are so imbued with the work ethic that they tend to denigrate children's play. Some even punish children for "horsing around," criticize teachers for letting children play "too much," or schedule their children's lives with lessons, homework, and chores so that there is little time to play.

Every age has its own special forms of play. Chapter 8 of the textbook differentiates play that captures the pleasures of using the senses and motor abilities **(sensorimotor play),** play that helps older children to master new skills **(mastery play),** and play consisting of the wrestling, chasing, and hitting that occurs purely in fun, with no intent to harm **(rough-and-tumble play).**

To increase students' awareness of the play and play needs of children, the exercise for Lesson 8 asks them to locate and observe play spaces near their home. They are then to answer several questions and return their answers to the instructor.

Since the pedagogical impact of this exercise is primarily based on students reflecting on their own observations, there are "correct" answers only for question 3 (examples of different types of play). This being the case, a substantial follow-up by the instructor is probably unnecessary. If desired, however, students could be asked to consider the following questions: In what ways does a child's history of play influence the rest of his or her life story? How is childhood play viewed by our society today? Is play encouraged, merely tolerated, or considered frivolous? How does this compare with how play is viewed in other countries or cultures you are familiar with? Have there been historical changes in the way society views play? How is play different now than when you were a child?

AUDIO TESTBANK

Note: A testbank for the text is published separately by Worth Publishers, Inc.

Multiple Choice Questions

The correct answer to each question is identified by a capital letter.

1. Compared to other primates, humans have a period of childhood that is:
   a. much shorter.
   b. somewhat shorter.
   c. somewhat longer.
   D. much longer.

2. In the first months of life, sex hormones in the human infant are:
   a. very low.
   B. as high as they will be during puberty.

    c. higher than they will be during puberty.
    d. nonexistent; sex hormone production does not begin until puberty.

3. Which of the following is suggested in the program as a possible reason for childhood's duration in our species?
    A. Delaying physical maturity and reproduction allows more time for learning.
    b. Remaining a child as long as possible reduces the risk of premature death due to accidents, fighting, and other adult hazards.
    c. Childhood is lengthened to compensate for our relatively short gestation period.
    d. All of the above are suggested.

4. The primary male sex hormone is:
    a. estrogen.
    B. testosterone.
    c. adrenaline.
    d. noradrenaline.

5. The primary female sex hormone is:
    A. estrogen.
    b. testosterone.
    c. adrenaline.
    d. noradrenaline.

6. According to experts in the program, the present duration of childhood in humans may have evolved because:
    a. of random variation in our species' gene pool.
    b. the daily demands of life faced by our hunter-gatherer ancestors necessitated shortening childhood so that physical maturity was attained as soon as possible.
    C. babysitting by older children conferred such an advantage to our species that our biological clock evolved to keep childhood as lengthy as possible.
    d. walking upright, which requires slow physical growth of the muscular-skeletal system, conveyed a reproductive advantage to our species.

7. A basic principle of physical development is that it proceeds:
    a. "outside in."
    b. "up and in."
    c. "from the bottom up."
    D. "down and out."

8. Children begin to understand and play games with rules at about what age?
    a. 2 to 3 years
    B. 5 to 7 years
    c. 9 to 11 years
    d. 13 to 15 years

9. According to Erik Erikson, the basic task of childhood is to develop a sense of:
    a. basic trust.
    b. initiative.
    C. industry.
    d. integrity.

10. In most mammals, the potential for learning and flexibility in behavior is greatly reduced when:
    a. early experiences prove frustrating.
    B. sexual maturity is attained.
    c. behaviors are too frequently reinforced.
    d. sex hormone levels are low.

11. In humans, "how to" time is also a time when:
    A. sex hormone levels are very low.
    b. sex hormone levels are very high.
    c. cognitive immaturity makes pretend play unlikely.
    d. boys and girls do not yet separate themselves into same-sex play groups.

12. In human development, the program governing reproductive maturity is put "on hold" at about what age?
    a. 1 month
    b. 1 year
    C. 2 years
    d. 3 years

13. In human prenatal development, sex organs are formed and sex hormone production initiated by _____ months after conception.
    a. 1
    B. 3
    c. 5
    d. 7

14. Evolutionary changes become coded into the body when:
    a. individuals pass an acquired trait on to their offspring over several generations.
    B. they confer a reproductive advantage to individuals possessing them.
    c. more than one-half of the members of a species possess a trait.
    d. both male and female members of a species possess a trait.

15. One of the first ways children practice adult skills is with:
    a. mastery play.
    b. sensorimotor play.
    c. rough-and-tumble play.
    D. pretend play.

Essay Questions

1. Cite two possible evolutionary explanations of why humans have such a lengthy period of childhood. (audio program)

2. Outline normal physical growth during the play years, and account for variations in growth. (textbook)

3. Outline the relationships between brain specialization, language development, and handedness. (textbook)

4. Cite and discuss two arguments in the controversy concerning when children should learn to read. (textbook)

5. Differentiate between gross and fine motor skills and describe their development during the play years. (textbook)

6. Identify three kinds of play and the skills they develop. (textbook)

7. Outline the main similarities and differences in the physical development of boys and girls during the play years. (textbook)

8. Some parents are so fearful of their children suffering an accident that they severely restrict the children's play opportunities. What are some of the possible consequences of such restriction on development in the three domains? (textbook)

9. Your neighbor wants to know whether she should begin teaching her 4-year-old daughter to read. What advice would you offer her regarding the advantages and disadvantages of doing so? (textbook)

10. In the program, Professor Bogin states, "The standard explanation for why we delay reproduction is we have so much to learn." What does he mean by this statement? (audio program)

References

Erikson, Erik. (1977). *Toys and reasons: Stages in the ritualization of experience.* New York: Norton.

Smith, Peter K. (1984). *Play in animals and humans.* Oxford: Basil Blackwell.

These two books discuss play as an essential part of childhood development. Smith's book is a collection of articles on topics such as imaginary playmates and the costs and benefits of play.

The Play Years: Cognitive Developi

AUDIO PROGRAM: Then Sentences

OVERVIEW

Lesson 9 of *Seasons of Life* explores cognitive development in children between the ages of 2 and 6 years. Young children think and speak very differently from older children and adults. The most significant cognitive development during early childhood is the attainment of **symbolic thought,** which opens a whole new world of imitation and pretend play to the child. This, of course, is Piaget's viewpoint, and discussion of his influential theory of cognitive development begins Chapter 9 of *The Developing Person Through the Life Span, 2/e.*

The second part of the chapter deals with language development during early childhood. Rapid growth occurs in the use of language, including its grammar, vocabulary, and pragmatic components. Language is limited, however, by the **preoperational thought** of the preschool child: his or her thinking is not very logical and is based on an **egocentric** view of the world.

The chapter concludes with a discussion of factors that promote cognitive development during the play years, including the impact of quality **preschool education** on children today. Whereas children once almost always remained at home until about age 6, today most begin formal schooling at an earlier age.

Audio Program 9, "Then Sentences," focuses on language development during early childhood, picking up where Audio Program 6, "First Words," left off. With the expert commentary of psycholinguist Jill deVilliers, the program examines how children come to produce their first primitive sentences and then move on to produce more complex speech. Several principles of language development are discussed in the program, including the importance of the biological clock, the natural propensity that humans have to acquire language, and how children master the rules of grammar through active experimentation rather than imitation. The insights that developmentalists have gained by comparing the acquisition of **sign language** to spoken language are also discussed.

Throughout the program, the speech of preschool children is used to illustrate principles of language acquisition. Particularly illuminating are the audio "snapshots" of a child's speech recorded at various times during her first twelve years of life. The program opens with actual examples of how this child produced "first words, then sentences."

LESSON GOALS

1. To describe how preschool children think.

2. To outline the main accomplishments and limitations of language development during the play years.

3. To discuss why the play years are a prime period for learning, and identify the kinds of experiences that best foster cognitive development during early childhood.

LESSON 9 EXERCISE: PRESCHOOL LITERATURE

To help students better understand the cognitive processes of preschoolers, the exercise for Lesson 9 asks them to examine a well-loved children's book. Many characteristics of preoperational thought and language are reflected in such books. Suggested titles include the *I Can Read* books by Arnold Lobel, the *Amelia Bedelia* books by Peggy Parish, the *Mr.* books by Roger Hargreaves and, for younger children, books by such well-known authors as Maurice Sendak, Charlotte Zolotow, and Dr. Seuss.

After examining the book, students are to answer several questions and to return their answers to the instructor.

Most students will be able to identify several of the elements listed in the exercise. For example, those who choose an *Amelia Bedelia* book will find that the fun is based entirely on the main character's literal interpretation of her instructions. The *I Can Read* books are full of literal, egocentric, and animistic interpretations of the world (for example, talking rocks, a moon that follows an owl home and is not invited to dinner, and a character who, when told that spring is right around the corner, goes looking for the corner). The *Mr.* and *Little Miss* books by Hargreaves are good examples of centration in writing. For instance, when the author writes about "Little Miss Helpful" or "Mr. Uppity," he is taking advantage of the young child's tendency to focus on only one characteristic at a time.

Although this exercise should prove very interesting and self-explanatory to students, if the instructor wishes to, she or he might follow up students' assignments by summarizing the class responses, or providing feedback on the accuracy of each student's understanding of preoperational thought.

AUDIO TESTBANK

Note: A testbank for the textbook is published separately by Worth Publishers, Inc.

Multiple Choice Questions

The correct answer to each question is identified by a capital letter.

1. In most children, the first word occurs at about _____ of age, and the first two-word sentence about _____ of age.
   a. 6 months . . . 18 months
   B. 1 year . . . 2 years

    c. 8 months . . . 1 year
    d. 10 months . . . 3 years

2. Compared to the child's rate of speech development, his or her understanding of language develops:
    a. more slowly.
    b. at about the same pace.
    C. more rapidly.
    d. more rapidly in certain cultures than others.

3. That a child produces sentences that follow rules of word order such as "the initiator of an action precedes the verb, the receiver of an action follows it," demonstrates a knowledge of:
    A. grammar.
    b. semantics.
    c. pragmatics.
    d. phrase structure.

4. The stage of two-word sentences:
    a. lasts longer than the stage of telegraphic speech.
    b. has been demonstrated in chimpanzees using sign language.
    C. occurs at about the same time in children throughout the world.
    d. occurs at different ages among children in different cultures.

5. When preschool children create speech "telegrams," which of the following parts of speech are usually omitted?
    a. all nouns
    b. only concrete nouns
    c. verbs
    D. prepositions

6. The two-year-old child who hears her mother say, "The baby can see herself," would be most likely to create which of the following two-word telegrams?
    A. "Baby see."
    b. "The baby."
    c. "Can see."
    d. "See herself."

7. Upon hearing her two-year-old child's telegraphic speech, a mother is most likely to:
    a. repeat the abbreviated speech of her child.
    B. restate the child's idea in a complete sentence.
    c. tell the child not to use "baby talk."
    d. do all of the above.

8. Most cognitive psychologists view language acquisition as:
    a. primarily the result of imitation of adult speech.
    b. determined primarily by biological maturation.

c. a behavior that is entirely determined by learning.
D. determined by both biological maturation and experimentation with language's rules.

9. The two-year-old child who says, "We goed to the store," is making a grammatical:
   a. regularization.
   b. extension.
   C. over-generalization.
   d. telegram.

10. The reason that children around the world make similar errors in pronunciation at certain ages is that:
   a. the brain and nervous system are not ready for speech until about age two.
   B. the vocal tract is slower to mature than other organ systems.
   c. the auditory system is not able to differentiate the complex sounds of speech until about age two.
   d. all of the above are reasons for these errors.

11. Anthropological evidence indicates that in the evolution of our species:
   A. sign language preceded spoken language.
   b. spoken language is at least 10 million years old.
   c. spoken language preceded sign language, but did not become a preferred form of communication until about 100,000 years ago.
   d. the vocal tract became capable of producing the sounds of speech only about 10,000 years ago.

12. Studies comparing the acquisition of language in deaf and hearing children indicate that:
   a. deaf children babble at an earlier age than hearing children.
   b. using sign language, deaf children produce their first words earlier than hearing children produce their first spoken words.
   c. hearing children produce their first spoken words earlier than deaf children acquire their first signs.
   D. using sign language, deaf children produce their first words, and their first two-sign sentences, earlier than hearing children do.

13. Children acquire the grammatical rules of language:
   A. implicitly, by experimenting with language, rather than through explicit instruction.
   b. automatically, as a result of inevitable biological maturation.
   c. even before they produce their first understandable words.
   d. at their own developmental rates, depending on the language they hear their parents use.

14. Which of the following is an example of a grammatical overextension that a two-year-old might make?
   a. "Daddy not sleep."

      B. "I falled down."
      c. "Baby eat."
      d. "Car happy."

15. The parents of a two-year-old child who says "poon," "tanding," and "tee," instead of "spoon," "standing," and "tree," should:
      a. have the child tested by a speech pathologist for possible articulation problems.
      b. not worry unless these pronunciations persist beyond 2½ years of age.
      C. not worry, because such pronunciations reflect the slowly maturing vocal tract.
      d. have the child's hearing tested.

Essay Questions

1. Outline the course of language development during the year after the child's production of his or her first word. (audio program)

2. What evidence is there of a common timetable for language development determined by the biological clock? (audio program)

3. Describe the ways in which young children and adults speak to each other and how this interaction promotes the child's acquisition of the rules of language. (audio program)

4. Compare and contrast the state of readiness of the auditory system, nervous system, and vocal tract for language acquisition during early childhood. (audio program)

5. Explain how the cognitive potential of young children is expanded by the ability to use symbolic thinking. (textbook)

6. What recent evidence has led to revision of Piaget's description of cognitive development in the play years? (textbook)

7. Cite several factors that result in individual differences in the development of language skills. (textbook)

8. If you have ever attempted to learn a new language, in what ways was your experience similar to that of a preschool child attempting to learn vocabulary and the various grammatical rules of language? (audio program and textbook)

9. In what ways does the preoperational thought of the preschool child limit language development? In what ways does the preschooler's language development foster cognitive development? (textbook)

10. How important is the consistent hearing of grammatically correct and fluent speech to the preschool child's linguistic development? Explain the reasons you have given. (audio program and textbook)

References

deVilliers, Jill G. (1980). The process of rule learning in children: A new look. In K. E. Nelson (Ed.), *Children's language* (Vol. 2). New York: Gardner Press.

Professor deVilliers, who is heard on the audio program, discusses the process by which children master the rules of language. The volume also includes other pertinent articles.

The Play Years: Psychosocial Development

AUDIO PROGRAM: Because I Wear Dresses

OVERVIEW

Lesson 10 concludes the unit on the play years by exploring ways in which preschool children relate to others in their ever-widening social environment.

During the preschool years a child's self-confidence, social skills, and social roles become more fully developed. This growth coincides with the child's increased capacity for communication, imagination, and social understanding. Chapter 10 of the textbook examines these aspects of development and discusses several important influences during this season, including parental style, social play, and television viewing. The chapter also discusses sex-role development and the controversial theory of **androgyny.**

Audio Program 10, "Because I Wear Dresses," focuses on how children develop **gender identity** as boys or girls. Through the expert commentary of psychologists Michael Stevenson and Jacquelynne Eccles, the listener discovers that by the time children begin school they have developed a strong sense of their own gender.

The program also explores the issue of whether the psychological differences between the sexes are the result of biology or learning. Psychologist David Gutmann explains how sex differences in behavior change across the life span. Although some sex differences (such as aggressiveness) may have a biological basis, they may not be set for the entire life cycle. The finding that men and women become more alike in later life is discussed, along with the implication that there are different social definitions of masculinity and femininity at different ages.

LESSON GOALS

1. To discuss the development of the self during the preschool years.

2. To discuss the importance of play in the lives of preschoolers.

3. To discuss how various modes of family interaction affect children's development.

4. To describe the transformation of gender identity and sex-typed behavior over the life span.

LESSON 10 EXERCISE: GENDER-ROLE DEVELOPMENT

The exercise for Lesson 10 explores several issues in gender-role development, including the extent to which gender identity is a reflection of behaviors modeled by parents, historical changes in gender roles, and whether parents should encourage gender-stereotyped behaviors in their children. Students are asked to complete a gender roles quiz and compare their answers with those of a friend or relative who is in a different season of life.

After students (and their subjects) have completed the quiz, they are to answer several questions and return only these answers to their instructor.

An appropriate follow-up to this exercise would be a summary sheet of class answers to questions 2, 3, 4, and 5. (From question 1 the instructor can separate respondents on the basis of season of life.) The summary for question 2 might compare the average number of items in agreement with traditional gender roles (maximum = 16) for each season of life represented by the respondents. For questions 3 and 4, the percentage of students who did, and did not, feel that their parents were models might be reported. For question 5, instructors might report the percentage of students that felt parents should encourage traditional gender-role development in their children, and the percentage that felt other-wise. If the instructor chooses, the summaries could be accompanied by bar graphs and samples of explanations for answers.

AUDIO TESTBANK

Note: A testbank for the text is published separately by Worth Publishers, Inc.

Multiple Choice Questions

The correct answer to each question is identified by a capital letter.

1. Gender identity refers to:
    a. an individual's biological sex.
    b. whether an individual dresses in a traditionally masculine or feminine manner.
    C. an individual's sense of being male or female.
    d. all of the above.

2. Research studies have found that children have some understanding of their gender identity as early as _____ months of age.
    a. 6
    b. 10
    c. 12
    D. 18

3. A child who does not yet understand that by changing clothing or hairstyle one does not change sex has not yet attained the concept of:
    a. gender typing.
    B. gender constancy.
    c. gender identity.
    d. gender role.

4. Gender constancy is usually attained by the time children:
   a. master the concept of object constancy.
   b. reach age 2 or 3.
   c. lose their egocentrism.
   D. start to school.

5. Despite the fact that in terms of premature birth rates, birth problems and rate of development, _____ are the more vulnerable sex, they are often estimated to be _____ (more/less) delicate.
   A. boys; less
   b. boys; more
   c. girls; less
   d. girls; more

6. Compared to female babies, boy babies are more likely to:
   a. be born prematurely.
   b. suffer from birth trauma problems.
   c. show colic and non-rhythmic behavior.
   D. have all of the above characteristics.

7. Which of the following is a sex difference often found even during infancy?
   a. Girls are less easily cuddled than boys.
   b. Boys pick up the rudiments of language more rapidly than girls.
   C. Girls are more sensitive to faces than are boys.
   d. Boys show more rhythmic behavior than girls.

8. Which of the following explanations of male-female differences in verbal ability and aggressiveness is offered in the audio program?
   a. Boys and girls have different biological inclinations toward aggressiveness and verbal ability.
   b. Boys and girls receive social reinforcement for different behaviors.
   C. Both a and b.
   d. Neither a nor b.

9. In terms of sex differences in aggressiveness and verbal behavior, which of the following is true?
   a. Boys are always more aggressive than girls.
   b. Girls are always more verbal than boys.
   c. Both a and b.
   D. There is much more variation between individuals of the same sex than there is between the sexes.

10. Three- and four-year-old children are likely to:
    a. seek out playmates of both sexes.
    B. segregate themselves into same-sex playgroups.
    c. prefer playmates of the opposite sex.
    d. identify equally with both sexes.

11. Which of the following is offered in the program as an explanation of why children separate themselves into same-sex play groups?
    a. Children who are seen interacting with a child of the opposite sex may be teased.
    b. Boys and girls have different styles of play.
    c. Competition between the sexes occurs at every age.
    D. Both a and b.

12. In terms of styles of play, the play of girls tends to place greater emphasis on _____, while that of boys tends to place greater emphasis on _____.
    a. competition; cooperation
    B. cooperation; competition
    c. pretending; real situations
    d. real situations; pretending

13. David Gutmann believes that men are biologically endowed with a greater tendency toward aggression because:
    a. men are physically stronger than women.
    b. the loss of a given number of men is more threatening to the survival of the species than the loss of the same number of women.
    C. the loss of a given number of men is less threatening to species survival than the loss of the same number of women.
    d. due to hormonal differences, men are less fearful than women.

14. According to David Gutmann, a primary task of women in ensuring the survival of our species is:
    A. instilling in children a sense of basic trust.
    b. ensuring the physical security of children.
    c. modeling affiliative behaviors for children.
    d. all of the above.

15. According to David Gutmann, as men and women move beyond parenting into later seasons of life, gender differences in behavior:
    a. become even more pronounced.
    b. remain about the same.
    C. diminish as women become more assertive and men become more nurturant.
    d. are greater than individual differences within each sex.

Essay Questions

1. Describe the development of gender identity in preschoolers. (audio program)

2. Explain some of the gender differences that are usually apparent in the first ten years of life. (audio program)

3. Describe the points of agreement among psychoanalytic, cognitive, and learning theories regarding psychosocial development in early childhood. (textbook)

4. Identify and describe three styles of parenting and their consequences on children's development. (textbook)

5. Outline the benefits and possible harmful effects of television viewing on young children. (textbook)

6. Identify two serious psychological disturbances of childhood and outline the best means of alleviating them. (textbook)

7. Compare and contrast the three theoretical perspectives on sex-role development during the play years. (textbook)

8. Luis and Maria wish to raise their child so she is not exposed to traditional gender stereotypes in their home. Tell how they might structure this type of androgynous home. (textbook)

9. Your neighbor is very concerned that his children are watching too much television and will be adversely affected by the prevalent violence on prime time programs. What advice would you offer regarding sensible television viewing? (textbook)

10. David Gutmann has referred to the "unisex of later life." What does he mean by this statement? (audio program and textbook)

References

Doyle, J. A. (1985). *Sex and gender: The human experience.* Dubuque, Iowa: Wm. C. Brown.

Doyle's book explores many controversial issues in the development of gender roles and gender identity.

Gutmann, David L. (1985) The parental imperative revisited: Towards a developmental psychology of later life. *Contributions to Human Development, 14,* 31-60.

Professor Gutmann, who is heard on the program, discusses his theory of sex differences across the life span.

The School Years: Physical Development

AUDIO PROGRAM: Everything is Harder

OVERVIEW

Lesson 11 introduces the season of middle childhood, the school years from 7 to 11, when growth for most children is smooth and uneventful. Physical maturation coupled with practice enables children to master many motor skills. Disease and death are less likely during this season than in any other.

Chapter 11 of the textbook outlines physical development during middle childhood. Although malnutrition limits the growth of children in some regions of the world, most of the variation in physical development in North America is attributable to heredity. Diet does exert its influence, however, by interacting with heredity, activity level, and other factors to promote **obesity**—the most serious growth problem during middle childhood in North America.

The textbook also explores the special needs of children with physical and educational handicaps, concluding with an evaluation of the advantages and disadvantages of educational **mainstreaming** to both normal children and those with special needs.

Audio Program 11, "Everything is Harder," introduces Sean Miller and Jenny Hamburg, each of whom is disabled by **cerebral palsy.** Their stories, illuminated by the commentary of physical rehabilitation specialist Dr. Virginia Nelson, illustrate that when physical development doesn't go as planned, everything is "off-time" and harder for all concerned. For **disabled** children, **handicapped** by the world around them, nothing—neither getting around nor meeting the ordinary developmental tasks of life—comes easily.

LESSON GOALS

1. To describe patterns of normal physical development and motor skill acquisition during the school years.

2. To explain the means for preventing and treating childhood obesity.

3. To explain the advantages and disadvantages of mainstreaming disabled children.

4. To discuss the ways in which meeting the developmental tasks of life is more difficult for children with disabilities.

LESSON 11 EXERCISE: EVERYTHING IS HARDER

Throughout the series, the development theory of Erik Erikson has been discussed as a useful model for studying life-span changes. Erikson's theory identifies eight important psychosocial crises in life, each of which can be resolved in either a positive, growth-promoting way, or in a negative manner that disrupts healthy development.

The exercise for Lesson 11 asks students to reflect on Erikson's stages of development and the special difficulties of disabled persons in developing a positive outcome to each psychosocial crisis.

Although Lesson 11 focuses on development during middle childhood, this exercise requires students to integrate material from earlier seasons of life and to anticipate developmental issues in later seasons. The instructor might check students' answers for evidence of understanding of each psychosocial crisis and a plausible example of how a disability might disrupt development. Suggested answer guidelines are given below. These could be provided as instructor feedback, after students have submitted their answers.

- During the first stage (trust vs. mistrust), babies learn either to trust or to mistrust that others will care for their basic needs. In the program, the story of Wanda Miller illustrates how a disability might make it more difficult for children to develop basic trust. When she first learned that her child was disabled, Miller had difficulty becoming attached to him—a temporary rejection that might have impaired the formation of trust in the child.

- During the second and third years of life (autonomy vs. shame and doubt), children learn either to be self-sufficient in many activities, or to doubt their own abilities. In the program it is noted that disabled children often are more dependent on their parents for a longer time than able-bodied children. Not having the skills needed to control their environments, disabled children may have more difficulty developing independence.

- During the third stage (initiative vs. guilt), children begin to envisage goals and to undertake many adultlike activities, sometimes experiencing guilt as they overstep limits set by parents. Although all parents are worried the first time their child tries a new activity, initiative may be particularly problematic for disabled children because "letting go" and permitting them to try new things may be more difficult for their parents.

- During the years from 6 to 12 (industry vs. inferiority), children busily learn to feel useful and productive; failing that, they feel inferior and unable to do anything well. Because things are often harder for disabled children they may need extra self-confidence, self-esteem, and persistence in order to feel good about their productivity.

- At adolescence (identity vs. role confusion), individuals establish sexual, ethnic, and career identities or become confused about who they are. Forming a positive identity may be harder for the disabled person because there are very few good role models with physical disabilities.

- Young adults (intimacy vs. isolation) seek companionship and love from another person, or become isolated from others. This stage may be difficult for the disabled person because of society's emphasis on external appearance and the tendency of people to choose partners on the basis of physical characteristics.

- Middle aged adults (generativity vs. stagnation) feel productive in their work and family or become stagnant and self-absorbed. As Jenny Hamburg stated in the program, "I'd like to have a family—three kids, a cat, a dog, a garden. What I want, basically, is what everyone else considers a normal life. And for me, that's one of the things I'm not sure whether I'll ever have."

- Older adults (integrity vs. despair) try to make sense out of their lives, seeing life as meaningful or despairing at goals never attained. Attaining a sense of personal integrity may be more difficult for the disabled person simply because a positive resolution to each of the earlier crises of life is more difficult.

AUDIO TESTBANK

Note: A testbank for the text is published separately by Worth Publishers, Inc.

Multiple Choice Questions

The correct answer to each question is identified by a capital letter.

1. Cerebral palsy is:
   a. a speech disorder that results from childhood infection.
   b. a cognitive disorder caused by prenatal exposure to addictive drugs.
   C. a movement disorder caused by brain injury.
   d. a growth disorder caused by childhood malnutrition.

2. One obstacle to identity formation in the physically disabled is:
   A. the scarcity of good role models with physical disabilities.
   b. the tendency of disabled people to isolate themselves from others.
   c. the tendency of disabled people to avoid confronting their feelings.
   d. the tendency of able-bodied people to treat the physically disabled as mentally disabled.

3. When parents learn that their child is disabled they may mourn the death of their dream of a normal child. According to experts in the program, this:
   a. indicates that family relationships may never be healthy.
   B. is a common, and normal, reaction.
   c. is a sign of immaturity in the parents.
   d. is more likely in young, uneducated parents.

4. According to experts in the program, the most difficult age for a disabled person to adjust to is:
   a. early childhood.
   b. late adulthood.
   C. early adolescence.
   d. early adulthood.

5. As presented in the audio program, disability is to handicap as ＿＿＿＿＿＿ is to ＿＿＿＿＿＿.
   a. cerebral palsy; Down syndrome
   b. Down syndrome; cerebral palsy
   c. social impediment; physical impairment
   D. physical impairment; social impediment

6. Which of the following is *not* true of cerebral palsy?
   A. It is a progressive disorder.
   b. It may be accompanied by hearing or vision problems.
   c. It may be accompanied by mental retardation.
   d. It may be accompanied by seizures.

7. Disabled children may have more difficulty than able-bodied children developing:
   a. initiative, because parents have more difficulty "letting go" of a disabled child.
   b. autonomy, because they often are more dependent on their parents.
   c. industry, because it may be more difficult for them to perform motor skills and to feel successful.
   D. all of the above.

8. Disabled persons may have difficulty establishing intimate relationships because:
   a. they tend to be more cautious than able-bodied persons in expressing their emotions.
   B. choosing partners in our society is often based on external appearance.
   c. disabled persons often prefer not to interact socially with able-bodied persons.
   d. of all of the above reasons.

9. Regarding the impact of a physical disability on the resolution of Erikson's eight developmental crises, which of the following is true?
   a. Disabilities hinder development mostly during childhood.
   b. Disabilities hinder development mostly during adulthood.
   C. A disability may make it more difficult to develop a positive outcome for each crisis.
   d. Disabilities usually have very little impact on psychosocial development.

10. Because parents of disabled children may have difficulty "letting go" of their children and permitting them to try new things, the children may have difficulty establishing:
    A. autonomy.
    b. initiative.
    c. industry.
    d. competence.

11. In the audio program, Sean Miller and Jenny Hamburg were disabled by:
    a. epilepsy.
    b. Huntington's disease.
    c. Parkinson's disease.
    D. cerebral palsy.

12. Of the following, which was *not* cited in the program as an obstacle to development faced by disabled children?

    a. Because they often take longer at activities, disabled children may have to choose between enjoyable activities.

    b. Disabled children have few good role models who are disabled.

    C. Disabled children face different developmental tasks than other children.

    d. Each of the above was cited as an obstacle.

13. Approximately one out of every _____ American schoolchildren is restricted by learning or emotional disabilities; by vision, hearing, or speech problems; or by an inability to use their limbs normally.

    a. 5

    B. 8

    c. 10

    d. 15

14. In the audio program, Sean Miller's cerebral palsy was caused by:

    A. the stopping of his heart during surgery.

    b. a family history of cerebral palsy.

    c. a high fever he contracted as an infant.

    d. his mother's use of addictive drugs during his prenatal development.

15. In the audio program, Wanda Miller's grief and guilt over her son's condition made it difficult for her to form an _____ with her baby. As a result, according to Erik Erikson's theory, her son might not have developed the basic _____ that is the developmental task of this age.

    a. affiliation; intimacy

    b. affiliation; trust

    c. attachment; intimacy

    D. attachment; trust

Essay Questions

1. Identify the causes and characteristics of cerebral palsy. (audio program)

2. Differentiate physical disabilities from social handicaps and cite several reasons why development is harder for disabled children. (audio program)

3. Describe normal physical development during middle childhood and account for the usual variation observed among normal children. (textbook)

4. Identify several physical and psychological factors related to obesity in children. (textbook)

5. Discuss how obesity affects a child's development. (textbook)

6. Describe the development of motor skills (and note limitations) during the elementary years. (textbook)

7. Describe two different approaches to educating children with disabilities and note the advantages and disadvantages of each approach. (textbook)

8. Your sister and brother-in-law have just learned that their newborn child has

cerebral palsy. What advice can you offer them regarding the special developmental needs of their child? (audio program and textbook)

9. You are in charge of designing the physical education curriculum for a new elementary school in your neighborhood. What activities, sports, and play equipment will you organize? Explain your reasoning. (textbook)

10. Your neighbor's daughter is overweight and is often teased in school. What advice would you offer your neighbor to help her daughter lose weight and/or cope with her social problems, and why? (textbook)

References

Meisel, C. Julius (1986). *Mainstreaming handicapped children: Outcomes, controversies and new directions.* Hillsdale, N.J.: Lawrence Erlbaum.

Various chapters in Meisel's book discuss the history of the mainstreaming concept, and mainstreaming's advantages, disadvantages, successes, and failures over the past ten years.

The School Years: Cognitive Development

AUDIO PROGRAM: Piaget and the Age of Reason

OVERVIEW

Lesson 12 of *Seasons of Life* explores cognitive development in children between the ages of 6 and 11. Thinking takes a new direction during this season, as children become much more accomplished at learning, remembering, and communicating, partly because their cognitive processes become less egocentric and more logical.

Chapter 12 of *The Developing Person Through the Life Span, 2/e,* begins with a description of Piaget's theory of cognitive development during middle childhood, beginning with the **5-to-7 shift** from **preoperational** to **concrete operational** thinking. When this transition is complete, children are better able to understand logical principles as long as they are applied to concrete examples.

The textbook also discusses an alternative way to look at cognitive development—the **information-processing view.** This view places more emphasis on the ways in which children process their experiences. During the school years children become better able to receive, store, and organize information, in part because of their improved memory skills.

Linguistic development during the school years is also extensive, with children showing improvement in vocabulary, grammar, and **pragmatics.** Children enter a new phase of language learning: they are now able to benefit from explicit instruction.

The chapter concludes with a discussion of children with special cognitive needs during middle childhood. These include children with **specific learning disabilities,** those with **attention deficit disorder,** and **gifted children.**

Audio program 12 focuses on a description of Piaget's stages of preoperational and concrete operational thought. Piaget's famous **conservation** experiments are illustrated with children of several ages, with expert commentary provided by psychologist David Elkind. Several landmarks of the 5-to-7 shift are illustrated, including the gradual disappearance of egocentric thinking, and the emerging abilities to categorize, deal with rules, consider two dimensions of a problem simultaneously, and take another's perspective. Professor Elkind also discusses the concept of the **competent child** and why the efforts of some modern parents to accelerate their children's cognitive development may not only be futile, but indeed damaging in the long run.

LESSON GOALS

1. To describe how children's cognitive and language abilities change between the ages of 6 and 12.

2. To outline the information-processing view of cognitive development during the school years.

3. To discuss the logical structures of concrete operational thought, according to Piaget.

4. To discuss the possible causes and treatment of specific learning disabilities and the attention deficit disorder.

LESSON 12 EXERCISE: PREOPERATIONAL AND CONCRETE OPERATIONAL THOUGHT

According to Piaget, preoperational and concrete operation children think about the world in very different ways. The preoperational child (4- to 5-year-old) sees the world from his or her own perspective (**egocentrism**), and has not yet mastered the principle of **conservation,** the idea that properties such as mass, volume, and number remain the same despite changes in an object's appearance. The concrete operational thinking of 6- to 11-year-old children is less egocentric and demonstrates mastery of logical thought, including conservation, with tangible objects.

The exercise for Lesson 12 asks students to replicate several classic Piagetian experiments with a younger (4- to 5-year-old) and an older (7- to 9-year-old) child, using the conservation tasks described in the audio program and *The Developing Person Through the Life Span, 2/e.* Students are also asked to interview their subjects and look for examples of egocentric thinking.

Following the tests, students are to answer several questions and return their answers to the instructor.

As a follow-up to the students' responses, the instructor could summarize the class evidence for a shift from preoperational to concrete operational thought by comparing the responses of the younger and older children. Alternatively, several interesting examples of preoperational thought, not discussed in the audio program, may be introduced. One is *animism,* the tendency of preoperational children to attribute life to inanimate objects. The child may become distressed, for example, when a stuffed animal falls, fearing that it may have been hurt. Another is *artificialism,* the belief of children that they, or other people, have created everything in the world. Asked why the sky is blue, the preoperational child may respond, "Someone painted it." Students could be encouraged to look for these examples of preoperational thought and to reflect on the psychological impact of such reasoning on children.

AUDIO TESTBANK

Note: A testbank for the text is published separately by Worth Publishers, Inc.

Multiple Choice Questions

The correct answer to each question is identified by a capital letter.

1. Which of the following is an example of phenomenalistic causality?
   a. a child who believes that his or her parents cause all of the problems in the world
   B. a child who believes that raising a window shade causes the sun to rise
   c. a superstitious child who avoids stepping on sidewalk cracks
   d. the child who believes that thinking "good thoughts" will keep him or her safe from harm

2. Preoperational children are egocentric because:
   a. most children are very selfish.
   b. they have not yet mastered conservation.
   C. they do not realize that two different points of view can exist at the same time.
   d. they believe that by thinking a thought, it will come true.

3. Five-year-old Jill, who cannot understand why her father cannot feel her toothache, is showing:
   A. egocentric thought.
   b. centered thought.
   c. decentered thought.
   d. phenomenalistic causality.

4. Which of the following illustrates how a preoperational child might think of a parent's death?
   a. Death is a final, biological event.
   B. The person has gone away, but may someday return.
   c. Death is like catching a cold; the victim will soon recover.
   d. If you are bad, you may die.

5. Although Piaget believed that children could not take another's point of view before the age of _____, some contemporary researchers believe that children as young as age _____ can grasp this concept.
   a. 4 . . . 2
   b. 9 . . . 5
   c. 6 . . . 4
   D. 7 . . . 3

6. Contemporary researchers believe that the loss of egocentric thinking is:
   A. a more gradual transition than Piaget believed.
   b. a more abrupt transition than Piaget believed.
   c. caused by the attainment of conservation.
   d. occurring at a later age in children today.

7. The 5-year-old child who centers her attention on the height of water in a glass, and fails to consider the width of the glass, will probably fail a test of:
   a. egocentric reasoning.
   b. consolidation.
   c. classification.
   D. conservation.

8. The ability to follow two dimensions of a problem at once is a sign that children have entered Piaget's stage of:
   a. preoperational thinking.
   B. concrete operations.
   c. formal operations.
   d. sensory motor thinking.

9. A parent breaks a large cookie into two smaller ones, much to the delight of her 4-year-old daughter, who now thinks that she has more cookie. The child believes this because she fails to understand:
   a. classification.
   B. conservation of area.
   c. object permanence.
   d. egocentric reasoning.

10. The typical child will grasp the concept of conservation at about age:
    a. 4.
    b. 5.
    C. 7.
    d. 9.

11. Seven-year-old Jack is able to sort a pile of toys into three categories: things that move; things that are alive; and things that can be eaten. This task is designed to determine if Jack has mastered:
    A. classification.
    b. conservation.
    c. phenomenalistic causality.
    d. formal operations.

12. According to Piaget, a typical 10-year-old would be in the stage of:
    a. preoperational thought.
    b. formal operational thought.
    C. concrete operational thought.
    d. egocentric thought.

13. Conservation of area is generally mastered:
    a. before conservation of liquid.
    b. at the same time as conservation of liquid.
    C. after conservation of liquid.
    d. only when formal operational reasoning is manifest.

14. In the audio program, Professor Elkind suggested that:
    a. parents should make every effort to foster and accelerate their children's cognitive development.
    b. Piaget's description of stages of cognitive development has been refuted by contemporary research.
    C. it is a mistake for parents to hurry their children's cognitive development.
    d. with the appropriate environmental stimulation, children are able to progress through Piaget's stages at a much more rapid pace.

15. A gradual shift from preoperational thinking to concrete operational thinking occurs in children between the ages of _____ and _____.
   a. 2 . . . 4
   b. 3 . . . 5
   C. 5 . . . 7
   d. 6 . . . 8

Essay Questions

1. Identify the cognitive gains that come with concrete operational thought. In what ways is thinking still limited among children in this stage? (audio program)

2. Discuss some of the psychological and social effects of preoperational and concrete operational thought on children. (audio program)

3. Discuss how some of Piaget's ideas have been modified recently, and how the social revolutions of the past 25 years have changed parents' expectations of children. (audio program)

4. Cite several of Piaget's ideas concerning school-age children's thought that remain influential, and several that have been revised by contemporary psychologists. (textbook)

5. Outline and describe the stages of the information-processing theory. (textbook)

6. Describe language development during the school years. (textbook)

7. Describe four specific learning difficulties and discuss their possible causes and treatment. (textbook)

8. Would a 6-year-old child find it easier to tell time from a digital clock or a clock with a face and hands? Explain your reasoning. (textbook)

9. Do you think that parents today are hurrying cognitive development in their children more than parents did in previous years? If yes, why do you believe they are doing so? What are some of the potential drawbacks of rushing a child's cognitive development? (audio program and textbook)

10. Imagine that you are a school principal attempting to restructure the conventional elementary grades on the basis of Piagetian theory. In what ways would your goals, lesson plans, and methods of instruction differ for a "preoperational class" and a "concrete operational class?" (audio program and textbook)

References

Elkind, David. (1974). *Children and adolescents: Interpretive essays on Jean Piaget.* New York: Oxford University Press.

Elkind, David. (1981). *The hurried child: Growing up too fast too soon.* Reading, MA: Addison-Wesley.

Professor Elkind, who is heard on the audio program, presents an illuminating discussion of Piaget's theory of cognitive development and elaborates on an issue introduced in the audio program: Do adults do their children a disservice by attempting to accelerate their cognitive development?

The School Years: Psychosocial Development

AUDIO PROGRAM: The First Day

OVERVIEW

Lesson 13 brings to a close the unit on the school years. Lessons 11 and 12 developed the idea that from ages 7 to 11 children become stronger and more competent as they master physical and cognitive skills. Psychosocial growth during these years is equally impressive.

As discussed in the textbook, the major theories of development emphasize similar characteristics in describing the school-age child. They portray an individual who is much more independent of the family (as stressed by psychoanalytic theory); more open to environmental influences (learning theory); and better prepared to understand the laws and processes of society (cognitive theory).

Chapter 13 also discusses several potential problems during these years, including the impact of low socioeconomic status, divorce, single parenthood, and maternal employment on psychosocial development.

Audio Program 13, "The First Day," focuses on the universal experiences of children taking their first step outside the family. As children begin school they confront a much more complex social world than they have previously experienced. This world includes new authority figures and a larger set of peers who provide an opportunity for conversation, play, exploration, and the shared joy of friendship. Through the commentary of psychologists Steven Asher and Sheldon White, the listener discovers the richness of this world of school and friends, and its landmark status in the developing life story.

LESSON GOALS

1. To summarize three theories about the psychosocial development of school-age children.

2. To discuss the impact that peers and the social environment have on psychosocial development during middle childhood.

3. To describe the problems that may cause stress in middle childhood and factors that help alleviate the effects of stress.

LESSON 13 EXERCISE: FRIENDSHIP

One of the themes of Lesson 13 is that middle childhood is a developmental period centered on the child's growing inclusion in the wider social world beyond the family. This world is a complex social environment that includes a large set of peers at school and a smaller network of friends.

To help students apply the material from this lesson to their own life experiences, the exercise asks them to recall the social organization of their own elementary school days (or that of another person) and to answer several questions. Their responses are to be returned to the instructor.

Since there are no correct or incorrect answers to this exercise, instructor feedback on students' answers is probably unnecessary. The educational benefits students will derive come from reflecting on their own past experiences in the light of lesson content. Should a follow-up be desired, however, the instructor might ask students how their thinking about the importance of friendships changed after completing this lesson.

AUDIO TESTBANK

Note: A testbank for the text is published separately by Worth Publishers, Inc.

Multiple Choice Questions

The correct answer to each question is identified by a capital letter.

1. The brain attains approximately 90 percent of its eventual adult size by age:
   a. 2.
   b. 3.
   c. 4.
   D. 5.

2. According to Piaget, a five-year-old is on the threshold of what stage of cognitive development?
   a. preoperational thought
   B. concrete operations
   c. formal operations
   d. postformal thought

3. The tendency to move into a larger social world beyond the immediate family occurs in children between the ages of:
   a. 1 and 3.
   b. 3 and 6.
   C. 5 and 7.
   d. 6 and 9.

4. The tendency of children to move beyond their immediate families into a wider social environment:
   A. occurs at about the same age in all known cultures.
   b. occurs at a younger age in Western culture.

c. occurs at a younger age in European countries.

d. is unpredictable in terms of age of occurrence.

5. The Native American Indian rite of passage in which young children make a journey seeking their totemic animal is called the:

   a. totem journey.
   B. vision quest.
   c. bonding trip.
   d. origin myth.

6. English Common Law and Catholic Cannon Law recognize 6- or 7-year-olds as being in the first stage of adulthood by giving them:

   a. fewer outlets for childish behaviors.
   b. a finite period of time in which to learn the norms of society.
   C. their first adult roles and responsibilities.
   d. all of the above.

7. In the program, Professor White refers to the "agony and the ecstacy of human development." By this he means:

   A. in addition to the many joys, some aspects of growing up are painful.
   b. biological growth is a process in which maturation is attained at the expense of the death of billions of neurons.
   c. people become more inwardly reflective and philosophical as they grow older.
   d. developmental psychology is a profession which can be both rewarding and frustrating.

8. In terms of the settings of the three developmental clocks during the school years, which of the following is true?

   A. The biological and social clocks tend to be synchronized; whether the psychological clock is in sync too depends on the particular child.
   b. The three clocks are in synchrony.
   c. Only the biological and psychological clocks are in synchrony.
   d. Only the psychological and social clocks are in synchrony.

9. In discussing friendship, 9-year-old children in contrast to younger children will:

   a. deny that friends are important.
   b. state that they prefer same-sex playmates.
   C. stress the importance of help and emotional support in friendship.
   d. be less choosey about who they call a friend.

10. Experts believe that forming friendships:

    A. provides a basis of security, even for very young children.
    b. is of minor importance to psychological development in early childhood.
    c. is more important to parents than to children.
    d. is stressed too much by educators.

11. Approximately _____ percent of school children experience serious difficulty in their peer relationships.
    a. 1
    b. 5
    c. 7
    D. 10

12. Experts have found that rejected children:
    a. share a number of common personality traits.
    b. tend to come from large families.
    c. often are only children.
    D. are a very diverse group.

13. Most rejected children:
    a. are overly aggressive.
    b. are aloof and withdrawn.
    c. have parents who were rejected children.
    D. lack positive skills in forming friendships.

14. Children who have serious difficulty in peer relationships in elementary school:
    A. are at a greater risk of having emotional problems later in life.
    b. usually overcome their difficulty in a year or two.
    c. later tend to form a more intense friendship with one person than children who did not have difficulty earlier.
    d. b and c are both true.

15. Which of the following is most likely to be effective in helping rejected children form friendships?
    a. Explaining how important friends are to well-being throughout life.
    b. Painting a bleak picture of their current friendless plight.
    c. Grouping rejected children together in various activities so they befriend each other.
    D. Teaching them the skills of communication, cooperation, and conflict resolution they apparently lack.

Essay Questions

1. Summarize the cognitive and social skills of the 5- to 7-year-old child and describe the important transition that takes place at this age. (audio program)

2. Discuss the important role that friends play in the psychosocial development of school-age children. (audio program)

3. Discuss the plight of the rejected child during the school years. (audio program)

4. Compare and contrast three theories about the psychosocial development of school-age children. (textbook)

5. Discuss the major developments in social cognition that occur during the school years. (textbook)

6. Cite examples of the "society of children" and discuss its importance. (textbook)

7. Discuss the importance of competence and social support in helping children to cope with environmental stress. (textbook)

8. Your nephew complains that "nobody likes me in school." What can you suggest to improve his social skills and popularity? What kind of child tends to be popular? (audio program and textbook)

9. In what ways is the "society of children" today similar to, and different from, what it was when you were a child? Give specific examples of cohort effects, if possible. (textbook)

10. Your neighbor has complained to you that her school-age child has no sense of responsibility around the house. What examples could you offer of reasonable jobs the child could be responsible for? (textbook)

References

Asher, Steven R., and Gottman, John M. (1981). *The development of children's friendships*. Cambridge, England: Cambridge University Press.

This collection of articles on the importance of friendship to psychosocial development is edited by Professor Asher, who is heard on the audio program.

Adolescence: Physical Development

AUDIO PROGRAM: Changing Bodies, Changing Selves

OVERVIEW

Lesson 14, which focuses on the nature and consequences of physical development during adolescence, begins a three-lesson unit on development between the ages of 10 and 20—the season when young people cross the boundary between childhood and adolescence.

Chapter 14 of the *Developing Person Through the Life Span, 2/e,* takes a detailed look at the physical metamorphosis of puberty and explores such issues as dietary needs, eating disorders, and the effects of early and late maturation. It also takes a critical look at the traditional view of adolescence as a "stormy decade," noting that family, school, and cultural contexts are important factors in a young person's adjustment to puberty.

Audio Program 14, "Changing Bodies, Changing Selves," discusses the mechanisms by which the biological clock programs puberty. Dr. Inese Beitins, a pediatric endocrinologist, notes that the sequences of biological events at puberty are nearly opposite for females and males. Girls mature earlier than boys, but fertility comes late in their schedule of changes and early in that of boys. The possible meanings of this sex difference are explored by anthropologists Jane Lancaster and Barry Bogin, and psychologist Laurence Steinberg. According to one view, the difference was shaped by our evolutionary past, at a time when the biological and social clocks were in sync. Today, however, fertility often arrives a decade before the individual is accepted as an adult by society.

As the program unfolds, the listener discovers the changes associated with puberty contribute a new dimension to the ways adolescents think about themselves and relate to others.

LESSON GOALS

1. To outline the biological changes of puberty.

2. To compare the similarities and differences in male and female development during adolescence.

3. To discuss the evolutionary perspective on male-female differences in development during puberty.

4. To describe the possible problems faced by boys and girls during adolescence.

LESSON 14 EXERCISE: BODY IMAGES IN ADOLESCENCE

A major theme of this lesson is that the physical changes of puberty have a profound impact on our self-images. Most people are able to remember at least one event, attitude, misconception, or worry they experienced in connection with the changes of puberty: having big feet, being the first or last to experience menarche, having a small penis, worrying about acne, voice change, and so on.

In completing Exercise 14, students are asked to answer several questions which should lead them to recall their own intense adolescent interest in physical appearance.

If a follow-up to the exercise is desired, the instructor could provide a general summary of answers to the questions. Most students will have ready answers to questions about their "best" and "worst" features, as perceived in adolescence. Typically, they will recall that parents and others had different impressions. Many students may now feel that during adolescence they put too much emphasis on their physical shortcomings; they may have learned to accept and even exploit the ways in which they differ from the cultural ideal. If you have older students, you may be able to point out that the cultural ideal itself changes, so that a "worst" feature of one adolescent cohort (such as straight hair or large breasts) may have been highly valued by adolescents in another cohort.

AUDIO TESTBANK

Note: A testbank for the text is published separately by Worth Publishers, Inc.

Multiple Choice Questions

The correct answer to each question is identified by a capital letter.

1. The word "puberty" specifically refers to:
   a. the onset of menstruation.
   b. the first ejaculation.
   C. the complete set of biological changes that occur at the start of adolescence and culminate in reproductive maturity.
   d. biological *and* psychological changes that occur during adolescence.

2. During adolescence, the biological clock increases the pace of development by:
   A. restoring levels of sex hormones to the high levels during infancy.
   b. causing the release of sex hormones into the blood for the first time.
   c. inhibiting activity of the pituitary gland.
   d. causing the pituitary gland to enlarge.

3. The average age at which puberty begins is _____ in boys and _____ in girls.
   a. 9. . . .8
   B. 10. . .9
   c. 11. . .10
   d. 14. . .13

4. The "master gland" which releases hormones affecting the ovaries in girls and the testes in boys is the:
   a. adrenal gland.
   b. pineal gland.
   c. thymus gland.
   D. pituitary gland.

5. Which of the following most accurately describes the pubertal development sequence in girls?
   A. breast buds and pubic hair; growth spurt in which fat is deposited on hips and buttocks; first menstrual period; ovulation
   b. growth spurt; breast buds and pubic hair; first menstrual period; ovulation
   c. first menstrual period; breast buds and pubic hair; growth spurt; ovulation
   d. breast buds and pubic hair; growth spurt; ovulation; first menstrual period

6. Which of the following is the correct sequence of pubertal events in boys?
   a. growth spurt; pubic hair; first ejaculation; lowering of voice
   B. pubic hair; first ejaculation; growth spurt; lowering of voice
   c. lowering of voice; pubic hair; growth spurt; first ejaculation
   d. growth spurt; lowering of voice; pubic hair; first ejaculation

7. On the average, girls begin the pubertal sequence _____ boys and become fertile _____ boys.
   a. at about the same age as; earlier than
   b. later than; earlier than
   C. earlier than; at the same age as
   d. earlier than; earlier than

8. Today, in the United States, the average woman experiences her first menstrual period _____ the average woman at the turn of the century.
   A. about 3.5 years earlier than
   b. about 1 year earlier than
   c. at about the same age as
   d. later than

9. According to some anthropologists, the present-day male and female sequences of pubertal development differ because:
   a. males who did not become fertile until after they were physically mature were more successful reproductively than were those who became fertile earlier.
   b. fertile females who retained immature features for a while were more successful reproductively than females who did not.
   c. both a and b.
   D. being physically developed before being fertile conveyed a reproductive advantage to our female ancestors but not to our male ancestors.

10. Compared to previous periods in our species' evolutionary history, the biological clock that governs the physical changes of puberty:
    a. is more closely synchronized with the social clock.
    b. is more closely synchronized with the psychological clock.
    c. is more closely synchronized with both the social and psychological clocks.
    D. is out of sync with the social clock that establishes age norms for adult status.

11. Early physical maturation:
    a. tends to be equally difficult for girls and boys.
    b. tends to be more difficult for boys than for girls.
    C. tends to be more difficult for girls than for boys.
    d. is easier for both girls and boys to cope with than late maturation.

12. Late physical maturation:
    a. is equally difficult for girls and boys.
    B. is more difficult for boys than for girls.
    c. is more difficult for girls than for boys.
    d. is easier for girls and boys to cope with than early maturation.

13. After puberty, most boys:
    A. have a more positive body image.
    b. have a more negative body image.
    c. have the same body image they had prior to puberty.
    d. have a body image that will not change significantly for the rest of their lives.

14. According to experts in the program, the impact pubertal development has on girls:
    a. is more predictable than that for boys.
    B. is less predictable than that for boys.
    c. is more positive than that for boys.
    d. is more negative than that for boys.

15. In forming their body images, most adolescents are strongly influenced by:
    a. the number of siblings they have.
    b. their parents' body images.
    C. cultural ideals.
    d. their past sexual activity.

Essay Questions

1. Explain why, according to some anthropologists, the biological clock programs fertility to arrive late in the pubertal sequence for girls, and early in the sequence for boys. (audio program)

2. Contrast the effects of early and late maturation on boys and girls in today's society. (audio program)

3. Describe the sequence of physical growth during adolescence in boys and girls. (textbook)

4. Discuss the nutritional needs and problems of adolescents. (textbook)

5. Cite several factors that influence the onset of puberty. (textbook)

6. Compare and contrast the traditional psychological view of adolescence with findings based on recent research. (textbook)

7. Discuss research related to the long-term effects of early and late maturation, and factors related to a young person's adjustment to being physically "off-time." (textbook)

8. In the program, anthropologists offered an evolutionary perspective on male-female differences in pubertal development. This view explained why fertility arrives late in the pubertal sequence of females and early in that of males. Imagine these sequences are reversed, with fertility arriving late in the male sequence and early in the female sequence. What are some of the possible developmental consequences for the sexes if the tables are turned? (audio program)

9. The classic view of adolescence is one of a "stormy decade." Based on your own experiences during adolescence, those of your children, or a friend, does this characterization of adolescence make sense to you? Explain your reasoning. (textbook)

10. In the program, psychologist Laurence Steinberg states that "for girls, growing during adolescence is more of a kind of crap shoot" than it is for boys. What do your think he means by this statement? (audio program)

References

Katchadourian, Herant A. (1977) *The biology of adolescence.* San Francisco: W.H. Freeman.

A thorough description of the physical changes of puberty is presented, along with the biological mechanisms by which they are programmed.

Adolescence: Cognitive Development

OVERVIEW

Lesson 15 examines changes in cognition that occur during adolescence. As noted in the textbook, young people become increasingly able to speculate, hypothesize, and use logic. Unlike younger children whose thinking is tied to **concrete operations,** adolescents who have attained **formal operations** are able to consider possibilities as well as reality.

The cognitive advances of adolescence also foster moral development, as young people become better able to grasp the idea of laws and ethical principles.

Adolescent thinking has its limitations, however. As psychologist David Elkind notes in Program 15, "All Things Possible," adolescents often create for themselves an **imaginary audience** and **personal fable.** They fantasize about how they appear to others, imagine their lives as heroic, and feel invulnerable.

The program also discusses a new theory of intelligence proposed by psychologist Robert Sternberg, who believes a **practical intelligence** emerges during adolescence, in addition to the logic of formal thought. This type of thinking may also help adolescents develop a more realistic picture of who they are.

Perhaps most significantly, the logical, idealistic, and egocentric thinking of adolescence may represent a first step in the creation of a life story. Such is the view of psychologist Dan McAdams, who sees adolescence as a time when young people begin to figure out what makes them unique and to forge their identity. As they do, they create a background of **ideology** and write a first draft of their own life stories.

LESSON GOALS

1. To describe the cognitive characteristics of the typical adolescent.

2. To discuss the cognitive component of adolescent problems with sexual behavior and drug use.

3. To identify ways in which adults can foster mature decision-making by adolescents.

4. To discuss the significance of adolescent thinking in the formation of identity and the process of creating a life story.

LESSON 15 EXERCISE: LOGICAL VS. PRACTICAL INTELLIGENCE

One theme of this lesson concerns **practical intelligence** which is better suited than formal operational thought to everyday situations. It recognizes that for many problems no single correct answer exists and that "logical" answers are at times impractical. Some researchers believe practical intelligence reflects the greater cognitive maturity of adults as they reconcile formal thought with reality.

The following problems are designed to stimulate thinking about the difference between formal thought and practical intelligence. Examples of acceptable answers are provided for each question. These may be returned to students as a follow-up to the exercise.

1. In Program 12, several children were presented with a Piagetian conservation-of-area task. Five "houses" were arranged in different ways on two "meadows." In one arrangement, representing a town, the houses were clustered together in one corner of the meadow. In another, representing the country, the houses were scattered about the meadow. Children were asked whether the spatial arrangement of the houses would affect the amount of grass to mow. Would there be more grass to cut in the "town," or in the "country?"

    (a) What is the *logically* correct answer to this question?

    Answer: Because the spatial arrangement of the five houses does not alter the meadow area they cover, the amount of grass to mow would be the same in the town and the country.

    (b) Are there *practical* reasons that might lead one to think differently about this question? What are they?

    Answer: Mowing would be harder and take more time if the arrangement of the houses left many small spaces between the individual houses. Thus, it would probably require less time to mow the houses in the "town" and it might seem there was less grass to mow than in the "country."

2. A woman threatens to leave her alcoholic husband if he comes home drunk one more time. One week later her husband comes home drunk. What should the woman do?

    (a) What is the *logical* answer to this problem?

    Answer: Pure logic would dictate that the woman should leave her husband.

    (b) What is a more *practical* answer to this problem?

    Answer: One hallmark of mature adult reasoning is it is more socially centered and less egocentric than that of younger individuals. In studying the answers of preadolescents (age 9–10), adolescents (14–15), young adults (20–25), and mature adults (30 and over) to problems such as these, Labouvie-Vief (1985) found a progression from "automatic" logical responses with no awareness of other interpretations of the problem, to an integration of the "logical" answer with other possibilities.

Reference: Labouvie-Vief, G. (1985). Intelligence and cognition, in J. E. Birren and K. W. Schaie (Eds.) *Handbook of the psychology of aging* (2nd ed.). New York: Van Nostrand Reinhold.

3. Consider the following domestic scene:

    "Downstairs, there are three rooms: the kitchen, the dining room, and the sitting room. The sitting room is in the front of the house, and the kitchen and dining room face onto the vegetable garden at the back of the house. The noise of the traffic is very disturbing in the front rooms. Mother is in the kitchen and Grandfather is reading the paper in the sitting room. The children are at school and won't be home until teatime. Who is being disturbed by the traffic noise?" (from Labouvie-Vief, 1985)

    (a) What is the *logical* answer to this question?

    Answer: Based on the logical relationships embedded in the passage—that the noise is most disturbing in the front rooms, one of which is the sitting room in which the grandfather reads—the "correct" answer is the grandfather.

    (b) Are there *practical* considerations that might lead one to answer this question differently? If so, what are they?

    Answer: Researchers have found that when asked who is being disturbed by the traffic noise, college students almost always give the logically correct answer. Older adults, however, often perceive logical relationships which differ from those the experimenter is interested in and answer differently. For example, some might reason the grandfather could not possibly have been disturbed by the noise, as he would not have chosen to remain in a noisy room. Others might reply the grandfather may have been hard of hearing or at the particular moment, the noise may not have been very disruptive.

4. Describe or create a "real-life" problem in which the logical answer may differ from a practical answer.

    Answer: Students' answers should demonstrate an understanding of the distinction between the logic of formal thought and the more pragmatic, non-literal, and relativistic reasoning of practical intelligence.

AUDIO TESTBANK

Note: A testbank for the text is published separately by Worth Publishers, Inc.

Multiple Choice Questions

The correct answer to each question is identified by a capital letter.

1. In Piaget's theory, adolescent thinking represents the transition from _____ thought to _____ thought.
    A. concrete . . . formal
    b. concrete . . . postformal
    c. formal . . . postformal
    d. preoperational . . . concrete

2. Thinking that is capable of dealing with possible events in addition to actual realities is at which of Piaget's stages?
   a. concrete operational
   B. formal operational
   c. postformal thought
   d. preoperational thought

3. Adolescents often are idealistic and develop crushes on people they don't even know. This reflects their newly developed cognitive ability to:
   a. deal simultaneously with two sides of an issue.
   b. take another person's viewpoint.
   C. imagine possible worlds and people.
   d. see themselves as others see them.

4. Josh's feeling that everyone is looking at him reflects the adolescent's preoccupation with the:
   a. personal fable.
   b. egocentric viewpoint.
   c. mirror image.
   D. imaginary audience.

5. The adolescent fantasy of being destined for great things is embodied in the concept of the:
   A. personal fable.
   b. egocentric viewpoint.
   c. mirror image.
   d. imaginary audience.

6. One danger of the personal fable is that it may lead adolescents to:
   a. mistrust their peers.
   B. take risks, falsely secure in their feelings of invulnerability.
   c. assume no one understands them.
   d. isolate themselves from others.

7. The kind of thinking rewarded in academic settings is:
   A. formal operations.
   b. concrete operations.
   c. postformal thought.
   d. practical intelligence.

8. Robert Sternberg believes that some people possess _____ intelligence, which reflects the ability to function effectively in their everyday environments.
   a. crystallized
   b. executive
   C. practical
   d. fluid

9. According to Robert Sternberg, formal thought is not very useful for everyday problems because:
   A. such problems usually do not have clearly right or wrong answers.
   b. most people never reach the stage of formal thinking.
   c. most people are capable of thinking logically but are too lazy to do so regularly.
   d. of all of the above reasons.

10. According to Dan McAdams, adolescents' creation of a personal fable:
   a. is an unhealthy sign that may indicate a need for professional help.
   b. is a sign that they are experiencing peer rejection.
   c. indicates the need to acquire basic social skills.
   D. helps them begin to form their identity.

11. According to Robert Sternberg, one thing practically intelligent people have in common is they:
   a. are introverted.
   b. are extraverted.
   C. have made the most of what they are good at.
   d. tend to set fairly easy personal goals.

12. According to Erik Erikson, adolescence is a time for establishing a sense of:
   a. productivity.
   B. identity.
   c. intimacy.
   d. generativity.

13. Adolescent thinking is:
   a. capable of exploring possibilities as well as realities.
   b. idealistic.
   c. speculative and systematic.
   D. characterized by all of the above.

14. Which of the following is the best example of a personal fable?
   a. Sandy believes every boy she meets is fascinated with her.
   b. Claude lies about past experiences to impress his friends.
   C. Maria believes that she is destined for a life of heroism.
   d. Ramone becomes disillusioned when his religious convictions are severely tested.

15. Why might it be said that adolescent reasoning is flawed?
   a. Adolescents are notoriously illogical in their thinking.
   b. Adolescents tend to overextend their newly found logical powers to all situations.
   C. Adolescent idealism may lead to inaccurate perceptions of reality.
   d. Adolescent thinking is more egocentric, or self-centered, than thinking at any other age.

Essay Questions

1. Explain how the development of formal operational thinking influences adolescent attitudes toward family and society. (audio program)

2. Compare and contrast formal operational thought with practical intelligence. (audio program)

3. Discuss the significance of the imaginary audience and personal fable in the adolescent's formation of identity and creation of a life story. (audio program)

4. Outline Kohlberg's stages of moral reasoning and explain how these stages are related to cognitive development. (textbook)

5. Cite several criticisms of Kohlberg's theory of moral development. (textbook)

6. Identify the main issues related to adolescent sexual behavior and discuss some of the possible explanations for the high incidence of sexually transmitted diseases and pregnancy among teenagers. (textbook)

7. Discuss the use of drugs by adolescents and identify several reasons why adolescents may have difficulty making mature decisions regarding drug use. (textbook)

8. What kind of experiences would tend to foster the development of practical intelligence? How do these experiences differ from those that foster formal operational thinking? Do you believe that schools should place greater emphasis on practical intelligence? Why or why not? (audio program)

9. The title of Audio Program 15 is "All Things Possible." What is meant by this title? In what ways does this title represent cognitive development during adolescence? (audio program)

10. The relationship of moral reasoning to cognitive development is discussed in the textbook. Based on this information, do you believe 18-year-olds should be considered legally adults and be allowed to vote, buy alcohol, and assume other adult responsibilities? Explain your reasoning. (textbook)

References

Sternberg, Robert J. (1986). *Intelligence applied: Understanding and increasing your intellectual skills.* New York: Harcourt Brace Jovanovich.

Professor Sternberg, who is heard on the audio program, develops his concept of practical intelligence and explains how people can improve their intellectual skills.

Adolescence: Psychosocial Development

AUDIO PROGRAM: **Second Chances**

OVERVIEW

As discussed in Lessons 14 and 15, the physical changes of adolescence transform the child's body into that of an adult, while the cognitive changes enable thinking to take a more logical and practical turn. These changes set the stage for psychosocial development, the subject of Lesson 16.

Chapter 16 of the textbook focuses on the adolescent's efforts toward **identity achievement.** The influences parents and peers have on psychosocial development are examined in detail, as are the normal difficulties and special problems of adolescence. These problems include **delinquency, sexual abuse,** and **suicide.**

Audio Program 16, "Second Chances," examines the psychosocial challenges of adolescence, emphasizing the particular vulnerability of today's teenagers. This vulnerability is dramatically illustrated by the stories of two teenage "casualties" who took advantage of opportunities to change their lives.

Although many of today's teenagers are damaged by this tumultuous season, the image of the troubled adolescent as irretrievable is inaccurate. Psychologists Ruby Takanishi and Richard Jessor note that peer group pressure is often the trigger for problem behavior in adolescence, however, the socializing role of peers has many potential positive effects. These include facilitating identity formation, independence, and the development of adult social skills.

In the course of the program Takanishi and Jessor describe the interventions that have helped adolescents with troubled beginnings take advantage of "second chances."

LESSON GOALS

1. To describe the four identity statuses of adolescence.

2. To discuss the role of friends and peer groups in identity formation.

3. To describe the possible effects of various parenting styles on identity formation in adolescents.

4. To explain why early adolescence, the years from 10–14, is an especially critical time for young people today.

LESSON 16 EXERCISE: IDENTITY THROUGH THE SEASONS

Identity formation is a primary task of adolescence. Ideally, adolescents begin to sense their own uniqueness in the larger social world of which they are a part, but the development of identity is not confined to one season of life. Like the life story itself, it continues to unfold over the entire life span.

To help students apply this truth to their own lives, the exercise asks them to respond to the deceptively simple question, "Who am I?" They are to give ten definitions of their identity in terms of social roles, responsibilities, groups to which they belong, beliefs and values, personality traits and abilities, as well as their needs, feelings, and behavior patterns.

After completing the list, students are asked to rank each definition and assign it a number from 1 (most important) to 10 (least important), indicating its importance to the students' identity. They are then to rank the items again, based on their importance ten years ago.

An interesting instructor follow-up to this exercise would be to summarize the class responses, noting any systematic differences in how identity is defined at younger and older ages. If you make this analysis, make sure you control for the current ages of your students. Do younger students, for example, define themselves more in terms of careers and future goals? Older students in terms of family and generativity?

AUDIO TESTBANK

Note: A testbank for the text is published separately by Worth Publishers, Inc.

Multiple Choice Questions

The correct answer to each question is identified by a capital letter.

1. Early adolescence spans the years from _____ to _____.
   a. 8 ... 10
   b. 9 ... 11
   c. 9 ... 13
   D. 10 ... 14

2. In the United States today, approximately 1 in every _____ adolescents drops out of school, never to return.
   a. 3
   B. 4
   c. 6
   d. 10

3. Which of the following countries has the highest pregnancy rate among adolescents?
   a. Japan
   b. Germany
   c. England
   D. United States

4. According to experts in the audio program, approximately _____ percent of adolescents make it through the years of "heightened vulnerability" with little difficulty.

    a. 15
    b. 25
    c. 50
    D. 75

5. Compared to that in other developed countries, illicit drug use in the United States is:

    a. much less.
    b. a little less.
    c. about average.
    D. greater.

6. Many experts believe that today's adolescents, compared to previous cohorts:

    A. are confronted with much more serious and potentially damaging decisions.
    b. have neither an easier nor a more difficult time.
    c. actually have fewer problems.
    d. have about the same problems, but are less well prepared to deal with them.

7. The program suggests "heightened vulnerability" characterizes the years of early adolescence because:

    a. children are becoming physically mature at a younger age.
    b. during this span of years, adolescents' sense of being immune to danger peaks.
    c. there are more opportunities for and encouragement of risky behaviors, such as drug use and sexual activity.
    D. all of the above are true.

8. Concerning the age of onset of puberty, which of the following is true?

    A. In both sexes, puberty now comes at an earlier age than it did at the turn of the century.
    b. Puberty comes at the same age in both sexes as it did at the turn of the century.
    c. Puberty comes at a later age in both sexes than it did at the turn of the century.
    d. Individual variation in the age at which puberty begins is too great for historical trends to be identified.

9. In the audio program, Valerie's drug problem began to turn around when:

    a. she received treatment with a drug that produced an aversion to alcohol.
    B. her parents placed her in a drug treatment program.
    c. her boyfriend's death caused her to panic.
    d. her younger brother began taking drugs.

10. Regarding the dangers of being hurt by alcohol or drugs, adolescents:
    A. often feel a false sense of immunity.
    b. are usually unaware of how serious the dangers are.
    c. typically have a realistic picture of the dangers but simply don't care.
    d. none of the above.

11. In the context of the audio program, "retrievability" refers to:
    a. whether adolescent memories of early experiences are accurate.
    b. the long-term effects of poor parenting on children.
    C. the ability of adolescents to recover from problem behaviors, such as drug abuse.
    d. the age at which adolescents begin to accept full responsibility for their actions.

12. Biologically, children are maturing at a(n) _____ age than in the past; socially, it is taking _____ for them to attain adult status.
    a. older; more time
    b. older; less time
    c. younger; less time
    D. younger; more time

13. In the program, the turning point in Tony's problem behavior came when:
    a. he accidentally shot his stepfather.
    B. he deliberately got arrested and was declared a ward of the state.
    c. he awoke one morning with a hangover and couldn't remember what he had done the day before.
    d. his mother forced him to leave home.

14. According to experts on the program, approximately _____ percent of adolescents do not make the transition to adulthood very well and are considered "at risk."
    a. 10
    b. 15
    c. 20
    D. 25

15. The "no-man's land" years, when adolescents are physically mature but socially not yet accepted as adults, is:
    a. briefer today than in the past.
    B. longer today than in the past.
    c. briefer for girls than boys.
    d. briefer for boys than girls.

Essay Questions

1. Explain why early adolescence is considered a period of particular vulnerability for young people today. (audio program)

2. Discuss the issue of retrievability in adolescence. Who needs a "second chance," and who is most likely to receive one? (audio program)

3. Identify and explain the kinds of interventions that have helped adolescents to take advantage of second chances. (audio program)

4. Describe Erikson's view of the development of identity in adolescence. (textbook)

5. Describe four major identity statuses that are typical of adolescence. (textbook)

6. Define "rite of passage" and give examples of this process from both Western and non-Western cultures. (textbook)

7. Identify three significant problems experienced by today's adolescents, indicating their causes and how they might be alleviated. (textbook)

8. Do you feel that today's adolescents have a more difficult time making the transition to adulthood than people in your age cohort did? Please explain your reasoning. (audio program and textbook)

9. Some psychologists believe the moratorium in identity formation lasts beyond adolescence, and becoming a parent—and not graduating, marrying, or beginning a career—marks the transition to adulthood. Do you agree or disagree with this theory? Explain why you feel as you do. (textbook)

10. Which of the parenting styles identified in the textbook best describes the way your parents raised you? What effects did your parents' style have on your development? Which style of parenting have you followed, or would you be most likely to follow, as a parent yourself? Why? (textbook)

References

Jessor, R., & Jessor, S. (1977). *Problem behavior and psychosocial development: A longitudinal study of youth.* New York: Academic press.

Professor Jessor, who is heard on the audio program, examines issues in high-risk adolescent behaviors.

Early Adulthood: Physical Development

AUDIO PROGRAM: Seasons of Eros

OVERVIEW

This is the first of a three-lesson unit on development between the ages of 20 and 40—the period of early adulthood. Lesson 17 focuses on physical development during this season.

Chapter 17 of *The Developing Person Through the Life Span, 2/e,* notes that in terms of overall health, these years are the prime of life. Although physical decline progresses at the rate of about one percent per year, most changes go unnoticed.

Physical development during early adulthood is not without potential problems, however. **Drug abuse, eating disorders,** and **violent death** are more likely than at any other time. The chapter discusses possible causes of these problems, such as restrictive stereotypes of beauty and masculinity, and various means by which they might be prevented from occurring.

Audio Program 17, "Seasons of Eros," explores the changing meaning of sexuality throughout the life span. Expert commentary in the program is provided by anthropologist Jane Lancaster; psychologists Janice Gibson, June Reinisch, and David Gutmann; psychiatrists Robert Butler and Thomas Carli; and psychotherapist Laura Nitzberg. Throughout the program the listener discovers the life-giving force of eros manifests itself at every age.

LESSON GOALS

1. To describe the normal, age-related changes in physical growth, strength, health, and the sexual reproductive system that occur during early adulthood.

2. To describe three major behavioral problems of young adulthood and discuss their possible causes and prevention.

3. To discuss the changing meanings of sexuality throughout the seasons of life.

LESSON 17 EXERCISE: EROS IN THE MEDIA

The popular media, which often depicts sexuality, frequently portrays sexual themes and stereotypes targeted to certain age groups.

The exercise for Lesson 17 asks students to examine television, radio, motion pictures, novels and magazines for examples of advertising or programming with portrayals of various seasons of eros. Their choices may come from current media sources or their recollections of media portrayals in earlier seasons of their lives.

As a possible follow-up to this exercise, the instructor might summarize the class responses; this would be particularly effective for the modal portrayal of sexuality in each season. The instructor might also note that a number of studies have shown males and females are usually portrayed differently by the media, leading to the perpetuation of physical and sexist stereotypes. As indicated in the textbook, such restrictive stereotypes can have an enormous impact on development. Dane Archer and his colleagues, for example, evaluated 1750 photographs of persons appearing in magazine advertisements. With remarkable consistency, the photographs emphasized the faces of men and the bodies of women.

Students could also be asked to consider questions such as the following: In what ways are age- and gender-related stereotypes self-perpetuating? Is stereotyping more prevalent in some media than in others? Do you believe that traditional stereotypes are changing in contemporary society? Why or why not?

Reference: Archer, D., Iritani, B., Kimes, D., & Barrios, M. (1983). Face-ism: Five studies of sex differences in facial prominence. *Journal of Personality and Social Psychology, 45,* 725-735.

AUDIO TESTBANK

Note: A testbank for the text is published separately by Worth Publishers, Inc.

Multiple Choice Questions

The correct answer to each question is identified by a capital letter.

1. In the audio program, the desire for sexual pleasure is referred to as:
   a. libido.
   b. thanatos.
   C. eros.
   d. sensuality.

2. Regarding theories of human sexuality, which of the following is true?
   a. Most theories place greater emphasis on male sexuality than female sexuality.
   b. Most theories place greater emphasis on female sexuality than male sexuality.
   c. Most theories cover the entire life span, but fail to differentiate among the various seasons of life.
   D. No current theory of sexuality covers the entire life span.

3. According to information presented in the audio program:
    A. children are born with a capacity for sexual pleasure that pervades the entire body.
    b. sexual pleasure is a learned, rather than biologically influenced, capacity.
    c. children have a greater capacity for sexuality than adults.
    d. adults have a greater capacity for sexuality than children.

4. Research has shown that children have some idea of whether they're boys or girls as early as:
    a. 6 months.
    b. 12 months.
    C. 18 months.
    d. 24 months.

5. In defining eros, the audio program emphasizes that:
    a. sexuality increases over the life span.
    b. sexuality decreases over the life span.
    c. among the animal kingdom only humans are sexual.
    D. every season of life is sexual.

6. During the decade of the 30s, in age:
    a. eros is weaker than it was during adolescence.
    b. eros is stronger than it was during the 20s.
    C. eros is likely to become coupled with a desire for intimacy and settling down.
    d. eros is more focused on the genitals than at any other age.

7. It is estimated that about ⎯⎯⎯⎯⎯ percent of the population will eventually identify themselves as homosexual.
    a. 2
    b. 5
    c. 7
    D. 10

8. Which of the following is generally accepted by experts as being responsible for the development of a homosexual orientation?
    a. Growing up with gay or lesbian parents
    b. Growing up with a weak role model for gender identity
    c. An as yet unidentified factor in a child's social environment
    D. None of the above

9. According to experts in the audio program, an individual's sexual preference:
    a. is biologically determined.
    b. is learned.
    c. is fixed throughout life.
    D. may change over the course of life.

10. According to Dr. June Reinisch, children at age 5 or 6 enter a latent period of sexuality because:

    A. they become aware of society's discomfort with sexuality.
    b. they find the pleasurable urges of sexuality frightening.
    c. they have not resolved their Oedipal complexes.
    d. they are preoccupied with the task of starting school.

11. According to David Gutmann, sexuality during later adulthood:

    a. is focused primarily on the genitals.
    b. depends primarily on the individual's health.
    C. is diffused throughout the body.
    d. is focused on the mouth, as it was during infancy.

12. According to marriage therapists in the audio program, couples who never experienced a romantic "high" of falling in love:

    A. may have more difficulties later in their relationship than couples who did.
    b. tend to have fewer difficulties in their relationship because their decision to marry was less impulsive.
    c. tend to rate their marital satisfaction no differently than those who did experience such a "high."
    d. usually become intimate as a reflection of their need to establish independence from overbearing parents.

13. Many older couples report once their children "leave the nest" their sex lives:

    a. become less satisfying, although no less frequent.
    b. become less satisfying and less frequent.
    C. are better and more exciting than ever.
    d. are no different than before the children left home.

14. According to David Gutmann, eros would probably be most narrowly focused at age:

    a. 5.
    b. 10.
    C. 20.
    d. 40.

15. The best predictor of how sexually active people will be in their 60s and 70s is:

    a. their health.
    b. how satisfied they are with life.
    C. how sexually active they were in their younger years.
    d. whether they are married or single.

Essay Questions

1. Define "eros" and tell how its meaning changes from the beginning of life through adolescence. (audio program)

2. Discuss the concept of sexual orientation and how experts believe it emerges in the individual. (audio program)

3. Describe the ways in which the meaning and expression of eros change during adulthood. (audio program)

4. Describe the normal physical changes in growth, strength, and health that occur during early adulthood. (textbook)

5. Identify the early physical signs of aging and explain why most signs of aging go unnoticed for many years. (textbook)

6. Identify the age-related changes in sexual response that occur during early adulthood. (textbook)

7. In what specific ways might early adulthood be considered the prime of life? (textbook)

8. Identify the leading causes of infertility and discuss the possible methods of prevention and treatment for this condition. (textbook)

9. Many psychologists believe restrictive physical stereotypes of "ideal men" and "ideal women" contribute to the problems of young adults. Do you agree? Give an example of such a stereotype and the potential problems it creates for young men or women. (textbook)

10. In your estimation, why are the physical problems of drug abuse, eating disorders, and violent death more like during early adulthood than at any other time? Are these problems unique to the present cohort of young adults? Why or why not? (textbook)

References

Daly, Martin, & Wilson, Margo. (1978). *Sex, evolution & behavior*. Belmont, California: Wadsworth.

This interdisciplinary work on sexuality includes discussion of human sexuality, sex role development, and parental care.

Whitbourne, Susan Krauss. (1985). *The aging body*. New York: Springer-Verlag.

The text provides a comprehensive description of age-related changes in physical vitality.

Early Adulthood: Cognitive Development

AUDIO PROGRAM: The Development of Faith

OVERVIEW

Lesson 18 is the fifth in a sequence of six lessons that tracks cognitive development over the life span. The first two of these, Lessons 6 and 9, explored the acquisition of language. The next two, Lessons 12 and 15, presented the theory of Jean Piaget, which identified four stages of cognitive development, culminating in the logical thinking of formal operations. Lesson 18 moves beyond Piaget to explore other ways of thinking.

The commitments, demands, and responsibilities of adulthood often produce a new type of **postformal thinking** that is more adaptive, flexible, **dialectical,** and better suited than formal thought to the practical problems of everyday life. Chapter 18 of the textbook contrasts formal and postformal thought and also describes the stages of adult cognition proposed by K. Warner Schaie.

Thinking about questions of faith and ethics may also progress during adulthood, especially in response to significant life experiences, such as higher education and parenthood. Audio Program 18, "The Development of Faith," presents James Fowler's theory of faith, which outlines six developmental stages over the life span. Although Fowler's theory is not without its critics, its emphasis on faith as a developmental process rings true. Faith, like other aspects of cognition, may very well mature from the simple self-centered and one-sided view of children to the more complex, altruistic, and multifaceted view of adults.

LESSON GOALS

1. To describe cognitive development during early adulthood and the stages of adult cognition proposed by K. Warner Schaie.

2. To discuss the complexity of postformal thinking and moral reasoning.

3. To describe the relationship of adult cognitive growth to higher education and other significant life events.

4. To outline James Fowler's stage theory of the development of faith.

LESSON 18 EXERCISE: THINKING DURING ADULTHOOD

The exercise for Lesson 18 tests students' understanding of the material concerning formal and postformal thinking, dialectical reasoning, and faith by asking students to write answers to the following questions. Following each question is a sample answer. Students' answers to the questions can be checked to make sure they demonstrate an accurate understanding of the various types of cognition. If a follow-up is necessary, these sample answers may be returned along with an explanation of why a particular answer is incorrect.

1. There are many different kinds of problems that arise in daily life. Based on your own experiences, or those of a typical college student or person in your season of life, give an example of a problem likely to benefit from formal operational thinking. Why is a logical answer to this problem appropriate?

    Sample Answer: Any situation requiring scientific thinking, logical reasoning, or speculation beyond dealing with concrete reality would benefit from formal operational thinking. Such situations are commonly found in college examinations and tests of intelligence. Analogical reasoning, for example, requires the recognition of a higher-order relation between two lower-order relations. For example, the essence of the analogy ATOM is to MOLECULE as CELL is to ORGANISM, is the recognition that molecules are comprised of atoms, just as organisms are comprised of cells. Each lower-order relation specifies a part-whole relationship.

2. Imagine that you are a minister attempting to convince the members of your congregation to become more involved in the religious life of the community. Based on Fowler's stages of faith, what kind of appeal might be most effective with members at the stage of "mythic-literal faith?" with members at the stage of "individual-reflective faith?"

    Sample Answer: Individuals at the mythic-literal stage take the myths and stories of religion literally. The sermon might therefore quote from Biblical stories and respected texts indicating God will reward those who demonstrate commitment to the religious life of the community. In contrast, individual-reflective faith is not a simple matter of literal acceptance of one's religion or the beliefs of significant other people. Individuals at this stage are able to articulate their own values and establish a commitment to a personal philosophy. The sermon might therefore be designed to provoke personal reflection and clarification of the congregation's values by posing pertinent questions, such as, "What are your responsibilities as a member of this religious community?"

3. Dialectical thinking involves the constant integration of one's beliefs and experiences with the contradictions and inconsistencies of daily life. Give an example of the use of dialectical thinking in your own life, or that of a typical person in your season.

    Sample Answer: Dialectical thinking is exhibited when an individual is able to consider two sides of an issue at the same time and forge them into a synthesis. Kathleen Berger gives a clear example based on the aphorism "Honesty is the best policy." While most people would accept this thesis uncritically, the dialectical thinker also considers the antithesis: honesty can sometimes cause hurt feelings. The dialectical thinker is able to create a synthesis of these ideas by deciding that honesty is a valuable goal, even when it seems hurtful at the moment.

4. The idea that personal commitment is a hallmark of adult thinking is central to K. Warner Schaie's stage theory of adult cognition. Referring to these stages and your understanding of how cognitive development is propelled by life experiences, tell why being a parent fosters cognitive growth. In what ways might being a stepparent or grandparent influence cognitive growth? What other life experiences have influenced your own cognitive development?

Sample Answer: As the textbook notes, the life event of becoming a parent may cause a person to feel, think, and act "like an adult" for the first time. Parenthood encourages commitments to the larger social system and reflections on issues of importance to others beyond the self. Being a grandparent may offer additional insight into the meaning of life as a whole and locating one's place in the endless cycle of generations. In Schaie's theory, parenthood helps the person move toward the "responsible stage" and focus on family and others under his or her care.

AUDIO TESTBANK

Note: A testbank for the text is published separately by Worth Publishers, Inc.

Multiple Choice Questions

The correct answer to each question is identified by a capital letter.

1. James Fowler defines faith in terms of:
   a. each individual's sense of truth.
   B. each person's ultimate concerns.
   c. the moral principles acquired from one's parents.
   d. religious conviction.

2. A key principle in Fowler's theory of faith is:
   A. faith grows and changes throughout life.
   b. faith is most accurately described as a continuous, rather than stage-like, process.
   c. each stage of faith is exclusive to a given age group.
   d. faith, like cognition in general, develops in all people in the same way.

3. The trust and mutual love of the parent-child relationship forms the basis of:
   a. intuitive faith.
   b. mythic faith.
   C. primal faith.
   d. synthetic-conventional faith.

4. Fowler's theory divides faith into _____ stages.
    a. 3
    b. 4
    c. 5
    D. 6

5. Children who interpret the religious stories of their culture literally are in which of Fowler's stages of faith?
    a. primal
    b. intuitive
    C. mythic
    d. conventional

6. One hallmark of synthetic-conventional faith is:
    A. the individual forms beliefs based on an acceptance of the beliefs and values of people important to him or her.
    b. most people never reach this stage of faith.
    c. this often emerges during middle adulthood.
    d. this stage typically emerges during late adulthood.

7. Young adults who begin to question and doubt their faith as well as that of significant persons in their lives are in the stage of:
    a. conjunctive faith.
    b. mythic-literal faith.
    C. individuative faith.
    d. intuitive-projective faith.

8. The transition from conventional to individuative faith is often triggered by:
    a. leaving home.
    b. exposure to people with different values.
    c. an unexpected loss.
    D. all of the above events.

9. The audio program discusses the life span theory of faith that was developed by:
    a. Kohlberg.
    b. Gilligan.
    c. Erikson.
    D. Fowler.

10. The 40-year-old woman who is sure of her beliefs, yet recognizes there are inconsistencies in life and things beyond understanding, is probably in which of Fowler's stages of faith?
    a. mythic-literal faith.
    b. individuative faith.
    C. conjunctive faith.
    d. universalizing faith.

11. A key principle in Fowler's theory of faith is:
    a. the development of faith is lifelong.
    b. faith need not involve religion.
    c. the older people are, the more difficult it is to say a particular stage of faith is characteristic of them.
    D. all of the above are true.

12. According to Fowler, the stage of universalizing faith:
    a. is reached by very few people.
    b. often is found in people who lead lives of personal sacrifice in an effort to advance universal values.
    c. requires a readiness to relinquish the self as the vantage point from which valuing is done.
    D. is characterized by all of the above.

13. Critics of Fowler's theory argue that Fowler:
    a. fails to recognize faith may develop continuously, rather than in stages.
    b. focuses too much on religious faith.
    c. proposes stages of faith that for most people are unattainable.
    D. does all of the above.

14. Which of the following was *not* mentioned in the program as a criticism of Fowler's theory of faith?
    a. The idea that faith, or any facet of development, comes in stages is controversial.
    b. The idea that certain stages of faith are "higher," or "better" than others, is unacceptable to some.
    C. Faith is defined too broadly and ignores religious faith.
    d. The theory fails to consider the ways in which faith changes in response to life experiences.

15. Which of the following is the correct order of stages in the development of faith according to James Fowler?
    A. intuitive; mythic; synthetic-conventional; individuative; conjunctive; universalizing
    b. intuitive; individuative; mythic; conjunctive; synthetic-conventional; universalizing
    c. individuative; intuitive; mythic; synthetic-conventional; conjunctive; universalizing
    d. synthetic-conventional; mythic; intuitive; conjunctive; universalizing; individuative

Essay Questions

1. List and describe the six stages in the development of faith proposed by James Fowler. (audio program and textbook)

2. Discuss the relationship between cognitive development and faith. (audio program)

3. Cite several criticisms of Fowler's theory. (audio program)

4. Outline the five stages in cognition proposed by K. Warner Schaie. (textbook)

5. Contrast formal operational thought with postformal thought. (textbook)

6. Define dialectical reasoning and discuss the relationship between cognitive growth and moral reasoning. (textbook)

7. Cite several ways in which life events may foster cognitive development. (textbook)

8. Based on your own experiences, how does college education influence how adults think? (textbook)

9. In what ways does the moral thinking of adults differ from that of children? (audio program and textbook)

10. Many psychologists believe that life experiences are important in fostering cognitive development. How might this be true? What kinds of life experiences might promote cognitive development? What kind might limit cognitive development? (textbook)

References

Fowler, James W. (1981). *Stages of faith: The psychology of human development and the quest for meaning.* New York: Harper and Row.

James Fowler, who is heard on the audio program, outlines his influential theory of the development of faith.

Early Adulthood: Psychosocial Development

AUDIO PROGRAM: Not Being First

OVERVIEW

Psychologists generally agree that the meeting of two basic needs—which Kathleen Berger refers to in *The Developing Person Through the Life Span, 2/e,* as **affiliation** and **achievement**—characterizes the direction of development during adulthood. For most adults during this season of life, parenthood is the primary expression of achievement. Parenthood, however, has become much more complicated for many adults. Audio program 19, "Not Being First," focuses on the changing structure of the family in the United States and the impact of these changes on children and parents.

Although many people tend to form closely knit **nuclear families** consisting of a mother, father, and one or more children, the number of **stepfamilies** is increasing.

Stepfamilies come in a variety of structures, including two stepparents, each remarrying with their children living with them; a noncustodial parent who remarries a parent with children; and a single person marrying a custodial parent with children. These trends in the composition of family members in American homes have created new notions about the words "family," "mother," and "father." Unlike nuclear families, stepfamilies usually include children who are members of two households. Extra sets of in-laws and grandparents and the stress of the competition that often exists between a stepparent and the ex-spouse all serve to complicate family relationships.

In the audio program, Elaine Horigian, a clinical psychologist, and Helen Weingarten, a professor of social work, discuss the problems that stepfamilies face as the members adjust to one another. Many of these problems are illustrated by the case of Penny, Lyn, and Heather Beesley. Married for six years, both Penny and Lyn had had previous marriages that ended in divorce. As the program unfolds, the listener hears of Lyn's struggles to form a bond with Heather, Penny's daughter from her first marriage.

LESSON GOALS

1. To discuss the ways in which adults meet their needs for love/affiliation and work/achievement during early adulthood.

2. To describe how the structure of the typical American family has changed, the causes of these changes, and the problems faced by stepparents and stepchildren as a result of these complicated family structures.

3. To discuss the issues facing adults in selecting a mate, marrying, choosing a career, and parenting.

LESSON 19 EXERCISE: GENOGRAMS

The exercise for Lesson 19 requires the student to construct a **genogram** (generational map) of his or her family. Genograms are convenient ways of visualizing how the structure of the typical family has changed over the years. Genograms have also proven to be a useful tool to therapists and family counselors in stimulating discussion with clients and providing insights into their life stories.

In responding to the exercise, the instructor might summarize the patterns in the genograms submitted. For example, how many show step-relationships? What are the average number of intra- and inter-generational ties among relatives who are alive now? The instructor could return to students a summary of the genogram information plus a thought-provoking question or two. For example, students might be asked to think about the ways in which historical changes in family structure have had an impact on their family members, as well as themselves.

AUDIO TESTBANK

Note: A testbank for the text is published separately by Worth Publishers, Inc.

Multiple Choice Questions

The correct answer to each question is identified by a capital letter.

1. By current estimates, one in every ⎯⎯⎯⎯⎯⎯ children under 17 will at some time live with a stepparent.
   a. 2
   B. 4
   c. 6
   d. 8

2. Which of the following best explains the current rate of stepfamily formation in the United States?
   a. Since 1950 the divorce rate has dropped dramatically.
   b. Divorce rates began to increase during the 1960s and 1970s.
   c. Because people are living longer than in the past, the divorced have more opportunities to remarry.
   D. B and C are true.

3. During the 17th century, stepfamilies were ⎯⎯⎯⎯⎯⎯; this was due to the fact that ⎯⎯⎯⎯⎯⎯
   a. nonexistent . . . divorce was prohibited.
   b. common . . . divorce was also common.

C. common . . . most marriages were ended by death.

d. nonexistent . . . most marriages were ended by death.

4. According to experts, which of the following is good advice for a new stepfamily to follow?

 a. Realize that a stepfamily operates by different rules than does a nuclear family.

 b. Do not expect stepchildren to switch their loyalty from their nuclear family to the stepfamily right away.

 c. Expect it to take three to five years for a stepfamily to form a sense of "family."

 D. All of the above are good advice for a stepfamily.

5. According to counselor Elaine Horigian, it often takes children longer to relate to a new stepparent because:

 a. they become resentful toward them.

 b. they feel that they have been abandoned by their biological parent.

 c. they have experienced a loss as a result of death or divorce and become mistrustful of all adults.

 D. all of the above are true.

6. What impact does stepfamily living have on the newly formed couple's relationship?

 a. Research indicates that the bonding of the new couple within a stepfamily is no different from that within a nuclear family.

 B. In the midst of many competing relationships, the new couple may be forced to deal with some very difficult feelings right away.

 c. In most cases, because of the support of other members of the stepfamily, bonding is facilitated.

 d. Stepfamily living prevents the new couple from establishing as strong a bond as they would in a first marriage.

7. According to counselor Elaine Horigian, in the first stage of stepfamily living:

 A. everyone tries hard to "put their best foot forward."

 b. family conflicts are common as members experience feelings of fear, anger, resentment, and threat.

 c. family members remain aloof and distant from one another.

 d. there is no predictability from family to family.

8. The negative connotations attached to the word "stepparent" are expressed in the fact that the word "step" originally meant:

 a. sick.

 b. evil.

 c. danger.

 D. orphan.

9. Professor Helen Weingarten has raised several concerns about the long-range impact of stepfamily living. Which of the following is one of those concerns?

   a. Stepchildren have lower self-esteem than children raised in nuclear families.
   b. Stepchildren generally do not get as much attention from adults in their lives as do children in nuclear families.
   C. Stepchildren who are shuttled back and forth between two households often have too easy a way out of problems.
   d. All of the above are concerns that have been raised.

10. Concerning the development of children in stepfamilies, most experts feel that:

    a. stepfamily living can only have a negative impact on children.
    b. in virtually every case thus far studied, stepfamily living has had only positive effects on children.
    c. it makes little difference whether a child is raised in a nuclear family or a stepfamily.
    D. the long-term impact on children is not yet clear.

11. Which of the following best describes the way a six-year-old stepchild might feel regarding his or her parents?

    a. Because children at this young age do not think in terms of absolutes, they readily accept the possibility of having more than one mom and one dad.
    B. Because young children tend to think in terms of absolutes, they do not readily accept the possibility of having more than one mom and one dad.
    c. Younger children often confuse their biological parents with their stepparents.
    d. Younger children show more resentment toward stepparents than older children do.

12. Which of the following is true concerning stepfamilies?

    A. In most stepfamilies, it's the father who's the stepparent.
    b. In most stepfamilies, it's the mother who's the stepparent.
    c. Stepchildren are equally likely to live with stepmothers and stepfathers.
    d. Most stepchildren are in the joint custody of their natural parents.

13. Which of the following is a mistake commonly made by stepfamilies, including those heard on the audio program?

    a. Stepparents may expect to form close relationships with stepchildren too quickly.
    b. Stepfamilies may try to become nuclear families.
    c. Stepparents might overlook a child's loyalty to the parent who was there first.
    D. Each of the above is a common mistake of stepfamilies.

14. According to counselor Elaine Horigian, after an initial "honeymoon stage," newly formed stepfamilies are most likely to:

    a. avoid dealing with their true feelings.

  B. experience conflict as feelings of fear, anger, and resentment come to the fore.

  c. experience the greatest degree of satisfaction with family relationships.

  d. realize that they will never be the same as nuclear families.

15. In the United States today, approximately _____ percent of marriages are likely to end in divorce: of these divorces, approximately _____ percent will involve children.
  a. 25; 75
  B. 50; 50
  c. 25; 50
  d. 50; 75

Essay Questions

1. In what ways do **nuclear families** and **stepfamilies** differ? (audio program)

2. What are the three stages in stepfamily development described by clinical psychologist Elaine Horigian? (audio program)

3. Why is it that "Every person in a stepfamily has experienced a significant loss?" (audio program)

4. What are some of the long-range effects of living in a stepfamily? (audio program)

5. What are the basic psychosocial needs of early adulthood according to Maslow, Erikson, Freud, and other developmental psychologists? (textbook)

6. What are the stages in the process of mate selection? (textbook)

7. What are the stages of parenthood in the life cycle? (textbook)

8. Imagine that you are a family counselor discussing with a group of new stepparents the possible problems they can expect. Based on information presented in the audio program, what advice could you give them as they form their new families? What difficulties should they expect? What are some of the "dos' and don'ts" you would advise them to follow? (audio program)

9. What is a "typical American family" today? How has its structure changed over time? Discuss these changes, their causes, and whether current trends are likely to continue in the future. (audio program and textbook)

10. What are some of the negative effects that stepfamilies can have on children? What are some of the positive effects? Given the choice as a child, would you rather live in a nuclear family or a stepfamily? Why? (audio program and textbook)

References

Lamb, Michael E. (ed.) (1982). *Nontraditional families: Parenting and child development.* Hillsdale, N.J.: Lawrence Erlbaum.

  An excellent, scholarly resource for research on the nontraditional family, Lamb's book includes articles on the effects of divorce and remarriage on both children and parents.

Middle Adulthood: Physical Development

AUDIO PROGRAM: **Improving The Odds**

OVERVIEW

The biological clock, a metaphor for the mechanisms by which the body times physical events, determines the potential we have for long life. However, as the author of *The Developing Person Through the Life Span, 2/e,* points out, our longevity is influenced by many factors, including health habits, socioeconomic status, and how we handle stress. Audio program 20, "Improving the Odds," introduces the listener to Susan, aged 47, and Larry, aged 59, as they complete a life expectancy questionnaire designed by Diana Woodruff-Pak. Although the test obviously cannot predict how long Susan or Larry will live, it is a teaching tool that identifies factors likely to extend or shorten their lives. An abridged version of the questionnaire is reprinted as the the exercise for this lesson.

As Susan and Larry complete the questionnaire, it becomes apparent that certain factors related to longevity, such as how long one's ancestors lived and the presence of hereditary diseases, are beyond one's individual control. Factors that are controllable, however, can add or subtract at least 20 years from predicted life expectancy. These include body weight, cigarette smoking, alcohol consumption, exercise, regular physical examinations, and maintaining a socially integrated lifestyle with a network of friends and relatives.

When we hear Susan and Larry's final scores at the end of the program, we also hear what health practices they hope to change. Despite the inherent uncertainty of correlational research, scientists agree that there are many things we can do to live healthier and longer lives. Indeed, the evidence suggests that in many ways, today's adults are becoming more conscientious about taking care of their health, thus improving their odds of living a longer, more satisfying life.

LESSON GOALS

1. To describe the typical pattern of physical development that occurs during middle adulthood.

2. To explain the relationship of an individual's life expectancy to lifestyle, genetic history, health practices, and personality.

LESSON 20 EXERCISE: HOW LONG WILL YOU LIVE?

An abridged version of Professor Woodruff-Pak's life expectancy questionnaire is reprinted as the exercise for Lesson 20. After students have completed the questionnaire, they are to determine the number of years by which their genetic history, personal health habits, socioeconomic status, and social and personality characteristics changed their predicted longevity. This information, together with a determination of how their life expectancy varied with factors either under their control and those that are not, is to be returned to the instructor on the **Exercise Response Sheet.** To protect privacy, students should not be required to send in the actual questionnaires.

As a follow-up to this exercise, the instructor might encourage students to have friends or family members complete the questionnaire and then discuss the following questions:

1. Did completing the questionnaire encourage you or your subject to make any changes in your personal habits or lifestyle? If so, what are those changes?

2. Were there are variables that you were surprised to discover were related to life expectancy? Which ones? Why did they surprise you?

3. Are there any variables that did not appear in the questionnaire that you would also expect to be related to longevity?

4. What research methods might you use to determine whether such a relationship does, in fact, exist?

5. What are the strengths and limitations of the correlational method of research?

AUDIO TESTBANK

Note: A testbank for the text is published separately by Worth Publishers, Inc.

Multiple Choice Questions

The correct answer to each question is identified by a capital letter.

1. The ratio of males conceived to females conceived is about:
   a. 1 to 1.
   B. 120 to 100.
   c. 50 to 100.
   d. 2 to 1.

2. The average number of additional years males and females can expect to live is:
   a. less for women until about age 20.
   b. less for men until about age 20.
   c. greater for women until about age 40.
   D. greater for women than for men at any age.

3. Women are believed to have a reduced risk of cardiovascular disease due to the presence of the hormone _____ Men are believed to be at greater risk due to the presence of _____
   A. estrogen. testosterone.
   b. testosterone. estrogen.
   c. prolactin. adrenalin.
   d. adrenalin. prolactin.

4. If you want to live a long time, your best choice would be to pick, in order of importance:
   A. a long-lived mother, a long-lived father, long-lived grandparents.
   b. a long-lived father, a long-lived mother, long-lived grandparents.
   c. long-lived parents, long-lived siblings, long-lived grandparents.
   d. long-lived grandparents, long-lived siblings, long-lived parents.

5. Obesity increases an individual's risk of:
   a. heart disease.
   b. diabetes.
   c. stroke.
   D. all of the above.

6. Concerning the relationship between longevity and the consumption of alcohol, which of the following is true?
   a. People who never drink live a few years longer than light or moderate drinkers.
   b. Moderate drinkers live longer than light drinkers.
   C. People who never drink live a few years less than light or moderate drinkers.
   d. There is no significant correlation between longevity and alcohol consumption.

7. If there is a positive correlation between age and intelligence, it means that:
   a. getting older causes people to become smarter.
   b. getting older causes people to become less intelligent.
   c. both a and b are true.
   D. age and intelligence are related, but not necessarily in a causal fashion.

8. Which of the following is the most accurate description of the relationship between longevity and socioeconomic status?
   a. People with lower socioeconomic status tend to live longest.
   b. People with moderate socioeconomic status tend to live longest.
   C. The higher a person's socioeconomic status, the longer he or she is likely to live.
   d. None of the above; there is no correlation between socioeconomic status and longevity.

9. Based on Professor Woodruff-Pak's findings, which of the following individuals should subtract the greatest number of years from their predicted life expectancy?
   a. a married woman
   b. a married man

    c. a single, divorced, or widowed woman
    D. a single, divorced, or widowed man

10. The maximum human life span is about _____ years.
    a. 80–90
    b. 100–120
    C. 120–140
    d. 140–160

11. The greater life expectancy of females compared to males is probably due to a difference in the setting of:
    A. the biological clock.
    b. the social clock.
    c. the psychological clock.
    d. each of the three developmental clocks.

12. A pregnant woman who smokes cigarettes:
    a. can expect to live fewer years than if she did not smoke.
    b. is at increased risk for heart disease, stroke, and cancer.
    c. exposes her unborn child to the same carcinogens as those that enter her body when she smokes.
    D. All of the above are true.

13. Of the following, which is *not* associated with increased life expectancy according to Professor Woodruff-Pak's questionnaire?
    a. exercising regularly
    b. drinking alcohol in moderation
    c. obtaining regular physical examinations
    D. eating a diet low in carbohydrates and high in protein

14. Which of the following conclusions can be drawn from Professor Woodruff-Pak's life expectancy research?
    a. There is very little that people can do to increase their odds of a long life.
    B. There are many steps that people can take to increase their odds of a long and healthy life.
    c. Personality characteristics are not correlated with life expectancy.
    d. Socioeconomic status is not correlated with life expectancy.

15. Which of the following is a limitation of the life expectancy research as discussed in the audio program?
    a. It is based on correlational, rather than experimental, research.
    b. No one has followed individuals who have taken the test to see if life expectancy predictions are accurate or not.
    c. Many of the life expectancy questions call for subjective assessments on the part of respondents.
    D. Each of the above is a limitation of the life expectancy research.

Essay Questions

1. What is the difference in life expectancy for men and women and why do researchers believe that this difference is a biological rather than a social phenomenon? (audio program)

2. In what ways do **personal health habits** predict longevity? (audio program)

3. What does it mean when there is a **correlation** between two variables? (audio program)

4. What are some of the signs of physical aging that begin to occur in middle-aged adults? (textbook)

5. What are some of the ways in which stress influences health? (textbook)

6. What are some of the typical changes that occur in the sexual–reproductive system during middle adulthood? (textbook)

7. Discuss some of the limitations of the life expectancy questionnaire. What are some of the reasons why one should be cautious in drawing conclusions from this type of correlational research? (audio program)

8. Based on the life expectancy questionnaire, what is your own predicted life expectancy? What factors could you change to improve your score? For each of the following areas, state whether (and if so, why) you are predicted to gain or lose years: genetic history, personal health habits, socioeconomic status, social and personality characteristics. (audio program)

9. Discuss the ways in which vitality during young and middle adulthood affects later health, including the role of exercise, smoking, diet, alcohol, and Type A behavior. (audio program and textbook)

10. Do you think you will be subject to less stress in 10 years than you are now? Explain why or why not. (textbook)

References

Krantz, D.S., Grunberg, N.E., and Baum, A. (1985). Health psychology. *Annual Review of Psychology, 36.*

The emerging field of health psychology represents psychology's contribution to the field of behavioral and preventive medicine. In this article, three prominent health psychologists review recent accomplishments in their field.

Woodruff-Pak, D. (1977). *Can you live to be one hundred?* New York: Chatham Square Press.

A very readable book in which Professor Woodruff-Pak presents a more detailed discussion of her longevity research.

Middle Adulthood: Cognitive Development

AUDIO PROGRAM: What Makes an Expert?

OVERVIEW

Lesson 21 of *Seasons of Life* explores how intelligence changes during the adult years and describes the methodology developmental psychologists use to study these changes.

Chapter 21 of *The Developing Person Through the Life Span, 2/e,* notes that psychologists' concept of intelligence has changed considerably in recent years. The results of many early **cross-sectional** studies led to the widespread belief that intelligence was a single, fixed, entity that peaked during adolescence and inevitably declined during adulthood. These findings, however, were undoubtedly distorted by **cohort differences** in education, career opportunities, and social and historical contexts. More recent studies based on **longitudinal** and **sequential** designs point to the opposite conclusion: that intelligence is **multidirectional** and, in some areas, actually improves during the adult years. Some experts believe that while **crystallized intelligence**—defined as those abilities that reflect accumulated learning—may increase with age, **fluid intelligence**—defined as those abilities that make all types of learning easier—declines.

The chapter includes a discussion of **expertise.** As people get older, their intelligence often becomes **encapsulated** in specific areas or skills they have chosen to develop. At the same time, abilities that are not exercised may decline.

Audio Program 21, "What Makes an Expert?," focuses on the particular "intelligences" of a musical savant and a skilled surgeon. That a savant is able to become expert in one area yet remain severely retarded in others demonstrates that intelligence truly is multidimensional and can specialize very narrowly. In the case of the surgeon, we see that in addition to being more experienced than a novice, an expert is more intuitive and flexible in his or her cognitive abilities, uses better problem-solving strategies, and often processes information automatically. During the program, commentary is provided by psychologist Neil Charness and Professor of Surgery George Zuidema.

LESSON GOALS

1. To discuss the controversy surrounding changes in adult intelligence and the role of research methods in fueling that controversy.

2. To explain contemporary views of intelligence and contrast them with those put forward by earlier theories.

3. To discuss the complexity and plasticity of the development of intelligence during the adult years.

4. To describe the distinguishing features of expertise.

LESSON 21 EXERCISE: CREATIVITY

To help students take a broader view of intelligence, the exercise for Lesson 21 explores the relationship of creativity to intelligence. The term creativity is used to describe the behavior of individuals who are able to find novel and practical solutions to problems. Research has indicated that in persons with an IQ of up to about 110 there is a positive correlation between creativity and intelligence. Higher IQ test performance does not predict greater or lesser creativity with any degree of accuracy. Although a certain degree of intelligence is obviously necessary for creativity to be manifest, environmental, biological, social, and cultural factors are undoubtedly also important.

Two copies of an adaptation of the *Remote Associates Test* designed by Sarnoff and Mednick appear in the study guide. The test is based on the idea that creativity reflects an ability to see relationships among ideas that are remote from one another. Students are asked to administer the test to an older adult and a younger adult. They are encouraged to take the test themselves if they wish. Scoring is based on the number of correct answers and the time required by each subject to complete the test. After administering the tests, students are to answer several questions on the Exercise Response Sheet and return only this sheet to the instructor.

By completing the exercise, students should have a better understanding of the multidimensional nature of intelligence. As a follow-up to this exercise, the instructor might return to students a simple statistical summary of the average time to complete the test and the average number of items missed (or answered correctly) for the younger adults and older adults whom students asked to complete the test. The instructor could also list any frequently mentioned cohort differences that students believe would influence the measurement of intelligence.

Reference: Mednick, S. A. and Mednick, M. T. (1967). *Remote associates test.* Boston: Houghton Mifflin

AUDIO TESTBANK

Note: A testbank for the text is published separately by Worth Publishers, Inc.

Multiple Choice Questions

The correct answer to each question is identified by a capital letter.

1. In their areas of specialization, experts are more likely than novices to:
   a. devote conscious attention to all aspects of performing their skills.
   B. perform their skill with little conscious effort.
   c. have close relatives who are skilled in the same areas.
   d. change interests several times during their adult lives.

2. When psychologists use the term "expert," they primarily are referring to:
   a. a person who is genetically gifted in a certain area.
   b. a middle-aged adult who has at least 20 years of experience in a field.
   C. someone who is much better than others at performing a certain task.
   d. any of the above.

3. Which of the following is characteristic of expertise as defined in the audio program?
   a. an intuitive approach
   b. automatic processing
   c. an ability to recognize rare cases
   D. all of the above

4. Which of the following was suggested in the program as an important factor in musical savant John LaFond's special ability?
   a. his innate musical talent
   B. his having been immersed in music his entire life
   c. both a and b
   d. No explanation of LaFond's ability was offered in the program.

5. The abilities of a savant who is gifted in music but otherwise severely retarded illustrate that intelligence:
   a. is largely the product of heredity.
   b. is largely the product of learning.
   c. cannot be measured.
   D. can specialize very narrowly.

6. Theresa is a mathematician and Brad is a philosopher. It can be expected that, because of the different nature of their professions, Theresa will make her most significant career accomplishments _____ than Brad will.
   A. at an earlier age
   b. at a later age
   c. at about the same time
   d. There is no basis for predicting such accomplishments.

7. The "swan song" phenomenon refers to:
   a. the impulse that most people feel at the end of their lives to achieve a sense of integrity.
   b. the tendency of middle-aged adults to attempt to fulfill their dreams vicariously through their children.
   C. the tendency of older composers to compose shorter, simpler, more concentrated pieces of music.
   d. the tendency of those who are dying to deny their impending death.

8. Compared to novices, expert musicians have:
   a. superior short-term memories even for random sequences of notes.
   b. superior long-term memories even for random sequences of notes.
   c. superior short- and long-term memories even for random sequences of notes.
   D. no better long- or short-term memories for random sequences of notes.

9. "Grand master intuition" refers to:
   A. the automatic, flexible play of a chess master who bases his or her performance on extensive past experience.
   b. the "beginner's luck" that most people have when first learning a new skill.
   c. a general problem-solving ability that is closely linked to intelligence.
   d. the undefinable skill for accurate problem-solving that some people just seem to be born with.

10. According to the audio program, the most important element in the development of expertise is:
    a. heredity.
    b. open-mindedness.
    c. intelligence.
    D. practice.

11. According to the audio program's discussion of expertise:
    A. everyone has the potential to develop expertise.
    b. only a small percentage of the population develops expertise in an area.
    c. women are more likely than men to develop expertise.
    d. men are more likely than women to develop expertise.

12. A distinguishing feature of the expert is:
    a. the early age at which his or her skill became apparent.
    B. that an expert in one domain may well be a novice in other domains.
    c. his or her self-centered nature.
    d. all of the above characteristics.

13. A distinguishing feature of someone who is an expert is:
    a. having superior general intelligence.
    b. having above-average memory.
    C. an ability to recognize familiar patterns and situations from past experience.
    d. Each of the above is characteristic of experts.

14. Experts, such as skilled surgeons, often find that their basic skills and techniques:
    a. become less important to their work as their experience increases.
    b. deteriorate, unless they pay close attention to what they are doing.
    C. become almost automatic as their experience increases.
    d. were exceptional almost from the moment they began their careers.

15. Experts tend to achieve their greatest professional accomplishments:
    a. during their 20s.
    b. during their 40s.
    c. during their 60s.
    D. at different ages for different professions.

Essay Questions

1. Describe the ways in which thinking changes as a person develops expertise in a particular area. (audio program)

2. Discuss whether experts in different fields of specialization have different peak years of achievement and productivity during the life span. (audio program)

3. What evidence from research led to the widespread belief that intelligence declines during adulthood? (textbook)

4. What evidence suggests that intelligence increases during adulthood? (textbook)

5. Differentiate between fluid and crystallized intelligence and explain how each is affected by age. (textbook)

6. Describe the contemporary view of intelligence, which places emphasis on the multidimensional and multidirectional nature of cognitive abilities. (textbook)

7. Discuss the impact of individual differences, plasticity, and encapsulation on intelligence. (textbook)

8. Choose an expert with whose skill you are familiar, for example, an artist, teacher, athlete, or parent. Describe this person's skill, emphasizing how it differs from that of a novice. Identify any differences that seem to be related to age. (audio program)

9. Identify the age group or cohort to which you belong. Mention several experiences that differentiate your early education from that of the generation in school today. Focus on technology, educational philosophy, changes in society, and any other pertinent differences. (textbook)

10. Based on the concept of intelligence as multidimensional and multidirectional, what differences would you expect to find in your own intelligence 10 years from now? (textbook)

References

Charness, N. (1986). Expertise in chess, music, and physics: A cognitive perspective. In L. K. Obler and D. A. Fein (Eds.), *The neuropsychology of talent and special abilities.* New York: Guilford Press.

Professor Charness, who is heard on the audio program, discusses further distinctions between experts and novices.

Schaie, K. W., and Herzog, C. (1983). Fourteen-year cohort-sequential studies of adult intelligence. *Developmental Psychology, 19,* 531–543.

Professor Schaie, who was one of the earliest researchers to recognize the importance of cohort differences, discusses issues raised by the assessment of cognitive development during adulthood.

Middle Adulthood: Psychosocial Development

AUDIO PROGRAM: The Life Course of Work

OVERVIEW

Lesson 22 completes the series' unit on middle adulthood by exploring psycho-social development during this season.

As noted in Chapter 22 of the textbook, middle age is a time when re-evalua-tion of career goals, shifts in family relationships, and a growing awareness of one's mortality often lead to change and sometimes turmoil. Author Kathleen Berger discusses several developmental issues in middle age, including the so-called **midlife crisis** and the increased financial and emotional demands placed upon middle-aged adults who are "sandwiched" between their children and aging parents.

The chapter also explores career development during middle age, the topic of Audio Program 22, "The Life Course of Work." In the program, the stories of Mary and Dan illustrate how the life course of work has changed. Mary, 48, returned to college when the youngest of her children started high school. Sociologist Alice Rossi, who has done extensive research on the work and lives of women, offers an historical perspective on women like Mary, who return to school and then to work.

Dan, 56, has been a dentist for 30 years. Although he loves his profession, changes in the field have led him to cease recommending it to others. Professor of Business Stephen Lazarus, who has worked extensively with those threat-ened by occupational changes, discusses the impact of career crises on people and offers advice to working adults of all ages. During the program, the listener becomes aware of the dramatic changes that have occurred in the life course of work and, more importantly, the tremendous psychological impact these changes have on workers who confront them unprepared.

LESSON GOALS

1. To discuss psychosocial development during middle age and whether midlife is invariably a time of crisis for men and women.

2. To describe the ways in which family dynamics may change during middle adulthood.

3. To discuss the dynamics of career development during middle adulthood and the ways in which the life course of work has changed.

4. To evaluate the stability of personality throughout adulthood and discuss the normal "unisex" shift that begins late in middle adulthood.

LESSON 22 EXERCISE: THE UNISEX OF LATER LIFE

The textbook notes that as people get older, both men and women tend to become more **androgynous.** The sharp gender role distinctions of earlier seasons break down and each sex moves closer to a middle ground between the traditional gender roles. Androgyny was also discussed in Program 10, "Because I Wear Dresses," which focused on the development of gender identity.

To help students better understand the concept of androgyny, the exercise for Lesson 22 asks them to administer a test of androgyny—the **PRF ANDRO SCALE**—to two adults of the same sex but in different seasons of life. Or they may ask an older adult to complete the test "as you see yourself now," and "as you were during your early adulthood."

In scoring the tests, students determine separate Masculinity and Femininity Scores for each respondent based on answer keys provided in the Study Guide. They are then to answer several questions and return only those answers to their instructor.

As a follow-up to this exercise, the instructor might summarize the class answers to question 1, perhaps in the form of a bar graph with mean scores for masculinity and femininity and a simple statistical analysis. Was there a difference in the scores of younger and older respondents? An appropriate statistical test would be a Factorial Analysis of Variance, with age group (younger/older), sex of respondent, and subscale (masculinity/femininity) as factors. Without burdening students with the complexities of the analysis, the instructor could merely report whether masculinity/femininity scores did, or did not, tend to converge in older respondents, and whether trends toward androgyny were equally pronounced in male and female respondents.

AUDIO TESTBANK

Note: A testbank for the text is published separately by Worth Publishers, Inc.

Multiple Choice Questions

The correct answer to each question is identified by a capital letter.

1. Prior to World War II female employment:
   A. was largely restricted to young unmarried women.
   b. was such that, if a woman worked at any age, it was considered shameful.
   c. was more variable than it is today.
   d. was such that all of the above are true.

2. The return of large numbers of married women to the labor force in the United States began during the:
   a. 1940s.
   B. 1950s.
   c. 1960s.
   d. 1980s.

3. The need for married women in the labor force was the result of:
   a. a loosening of gender stereotypes regarding socially acceptable professions.
   b. a shortage of male workers during the Korean War.
   C. a shortage of unmarried women.
   d. all of the above.

4. The phenomenon in which large numbers of married women returned to the labor force is primarily an example of the resetting of the:
   a. biological clock.
   b. psychological clock.
   C. social clock.
   d. three developmental clocks.

5. Employers began hiring more married women in the 1950s because:
   a. there was a shortage of unmarried women.
   b. the gender stratification of jobs left them no alternative but to fill certain positions with females.
   C. both a and b.
   d. none of the above.

6. Today, approximately _____ percent of mothers with preschool children are employed.
   a. 10
   b. 25
   c. 35
   D. 50

7. Regarding an individual starting a new career in his or her 40s, experts in the program state:
   A. for many careers, 40 is probably not too late to begin.
   b. 40 is not too late to make a mid-career correction, but it is usually too late to begin a new career in most fields.
   c. those just beginning a career at any age are usually less productive than people who have been in the field for many years.
   d. most 40-year-olds lack the necessary patience to successfully start a new career.

8. According to experts in the program, one advantage older workers starting a new career often bring to their profession is:
   a. a greater concern than younger workers for the welfare of the company.
   B. greater energy than workers who have been in the field for many years.

    c. less of a need for establishing their personal identity through their work.
    d. all of the above.

9. Today, the odds of a person staying in one occupation for life are:
    a. about the same as in the past.
    b. a little higher than in the past.
    c. much higher than in the past.
    D. increasingly smaller than in the past.

10. Workers are most likely to change occupations during:
    A. early adulthood.
    b. middle adulthood.
    c. late adulthood.
    d. There is no relationship between age and the likelihood of a worker changing occupations.

11. Stephen Lazarus has found that losing one's job:
    a. usually is not as traumatic as most imagine.
    b. has a greater psychological impact on males than females.
    c. has a greater psychological impact on females than males.
    D. often threatens the worker's sense of identity.

12. Approximately what percentage of workers in the United States can be expected to change occupations at least once during their lives?
    a. 30%
    b. 60%
    c. 75%
    D. 90%

13. According to experts in the program, 40-year-old workers today can expect:
    a. shrinking promotional opportunities in the future.
    b. pressure from younger workers desiring to move up.
    c. a reluctance of older workers to vacate positions.
    D. all of the above.

14. Which of the following pieces of advice was *not* offered in the program to those making occupational choices?
    a. "Don't expect that your life will be neatly divided into three segments corresponding to education, work, and retirement."
    b. "Baby boomers should be prepared for shrinking career opportunities in the future."
    C. "Try to stick with the same job if you can, since those who do report the greatest satisfaction with their lives."
    d. "Before making an occupational choice, take a good look at people already employed in that job."

15. Which of the following patterns of occupational history is becoming less common?
    a. "Trying out" several career possibilities before settling on one
    b. Changing careers at midlife
    c. Breaking away from work periodically to acquire new skills
    D. A "linear" career of education during early adulthood, working until age 65, and retirement thereafter

Essay Questions

1. What historical, economic, and demographic factors have led to the return of large numbers of married women to school and the labor force? (audio program)

2. In what ways has the life course of work changed in recent generations? (audio program)

3. What advice is offered in the program for those making occupational decisions at ages 20, 40, and 60? (audio program)

4. Discuss the concept of midlife crisis and the evidence from research on its inevitability in men and women. (textbook)

5. Discuss the concept of the "sandwich generation" and describe how relationships between middle-aged adults and their parents and between middle-aged adults and their adult children change at midlife. (textbook)

6. Discuss the shift in career dynamics that typically occurs during middle age. (textbook)

7. Discuss whether personality traits remain stable throughout the life span. (textbook)

8. In your estimation is the "midlife crisis" more common today than in previous generations, or are we simply more aware of it as a result of media exposure? Explain your reasoning. (audio program and textbook)

9. What are some of the ways in which career dynamics change during middle age? How have career dynamics changed over the life span of the past generation? In what ways are they likely to change in the future? (audio program and textbook)

References

Gutmann, David L. (1985). The parental imperative revisited: Towards a developmental psychology of later life. *Contributions to Human Development, 14,* 30–60.

Rossi, Alice S. (1980). Life-span theories in women's lives. *Signs, 6,* 4–32.

Psychologist David Gutmann and sociologist Alice Rossi, both of whom appear throughout the *Seasons of Life* series, discuss issues pertaining to psychosocial development during adulthood.

Late Adulthood: Physical Development

AUDIO PROGRAM: Opening the Biological Clock

OVERVIEW

Since 1900 over twenty-five years have been added to the **life expectancy** of the average newborn. This is the largest increase of any comparable time in history and is probably the result of the elimination of **acute diseases** as causes of death. Although life expectancy has increased, **life span**—the biological limit of life—remains fixed at about 100 to 120 years.

How has this increase in the average number of years a person can expect to live changed our lives? Audio Program 23, "Opening the Biological Clock," and Chapter 23 of *The Developing Person Through the Life Span, 2/e,* are both concerned with the physical changes that take place during this lengthened season of late adulthood. As the textbook indicates, in a nationwide poll most people between the ages of 18 and 65 thought that the elderly spend much of their time doing very little. This **ageist** stereotype is inaccurate, but reflects the premium that our culture places on youthful strength and vitality.

Is the physical decline experienced by persons during their 60s, 70s, or 80s inevitable? In addressing this question, the program discusses the efforts of researchers such as biologist Richard Adleman and psychiatrist Robert Butler, who are attempting to unlock the mysteries of the **biological clock**—a metaphor for the body's many mechanisms of timing. Scientists are finding that many of the physical changes that accompany aging are not the result of the passage of time per se, but are due to chronic disease, social context, and other external factors.

As science continues to unravel the mysteries of the biological clock a number of fascinating questions are raised. Why do people die? Can the life span be increased? What effect will added years of life have on the individual? On society? As the shape of the **demographic pyramid** changes to reflect the increased number of elderly persons, these questions will become increasingly important to our understanding of this, the final season of life.

LESSON GOALS

1. To give a realistic view of the physical changes that are due to aging itself and those that are a result of social context, disease, and other external factors.

2. To describe the biological clock as a metaphor for the body's way of timing events, such as death, and examine several theories of why aging occurs.

3. To discuss the causes and effects of ageism.

LESSON 23 EXERCISE: AGEISM

The exercise for Lesson 23 requires the student to reflect on the textbook's distinction between the **young-old** and the **old-old**, a distinction based not so much on age as on characteristics related to health and social well-being. Textbook author Kathleen Berger notes that many professionals who work with the elderly have inadvertently fostered **ageist** stereotypes of late adulthood by focusing on the difficulties and declines of the old-old and ignoring the young-old who make up the large majority of the elderly.

In this exercise students are asked to think of two elderly relatives, friends, or well-known personalities who fit the descriptions of these two groups. They are to write brief statements describing the health, personalities, and lifestyles of these individuals, and to explain why they classified each person as old-old or young-old.

In responding to the exercise, the instructor might pose several thought-provoking questions for students to consider. For example, students might be asked whether most of the older adults they know would be described as old-old or young-old. Other interesting issues for students to consider are whether ageist stereotypes of late adulthood are accurate, why they persist, and whether they are changing. Students could also be encouraged to speculate on what experiences of biological, social, and psychological development might lead one person to become "old-old" and another "young-old."

AUDIO TESTBANK

Note: A testbank for the text is published separately by Worth Publishers, Inc.

Multiple Choice Questions

The correct answer to each question is identified by a capital letter.

1. Since 1900 over 25 years have been added to life _____ while _____
   A. expectancy... life span has not changed.
   b. span ... life expectancy has not changed.
   c. expectancy... life span has increased by about 15 years.
   d. span ... life expectancy has increased by about 15 years.

2. The 25 years of life added over the past century are probably due to:
   a. the resetting of the biological clock.
   B. fewer acute illnesses in older persons.
   c. fewer chronic illnesses in older persons.
   d. all of the above factors.

3. Researchers are increasingly discovering that many physical changes once thought to be intrinsic to the process of aging itself are actually the product of:
   a. disease.
   b. social context.
   c. lifestyle.
   D. all of the above.

4. Which of the following best explains the relationship between male sexual capacity, testosterone levels, and aging?
   a. Sexual capacity and testosterone levels decline as men age.
   b. Testosterone level, but not necessarily sexual capacity, declines in older men.
   c. Sexual capacity, but not necessarily testosterone level, declines as men age.
   D. Sexual capacity and testosterone levels decline only in older men who are segregated from women.

5. In terms of their similarity to others of their own age:
   a. older adults tend to have more in common than do those who are younger.
   B. older adults tend to have less in common than do those who are younger.
   c. older women have more in common than do older men.
   d. older men have more in common than do older women.

6. Which of the following features of the life span probably *is* intrinsic to aging?
   A. Behavior slows down.
   b. People become more and more alike as they get older.
   c. Interest in sex diminishes.
   d. All of the above are probably a result of aging.

7. Biologist Leonard Hayflick discovered that when normal human cells are cultivated in the laboratory:
   a. they will continue to divide forever.
   b. cells taken from older individuals will survive for a longer than normal time period.
   c. cells taken from younger individuals will survive for a longer than normal time period.
   D. they will reproduce a finite number of times and then die.

8. The "biological clock" refers to:
   a. the master gene in every cell that determines the moment of death.
   b. the evolutionary forces that have resulted in the present day life span and life expectancy of each species.
   C. the various mechanisms by which the body times physiological life events.
   d. the difference in years between an individual's life expectancy and actual life span.

9. Concerning the concept of "programmed death," most biologists believe that:
   A. specific genes turn off cell division and provoke cell death.
   b. a master gene, or other device determines the moment of death in each person.
   c. death is an accidental rather than predictable event.
   d. all of the above statements are true.

10. Which of the following best explains the relationship of aging to the incidence of acute and chronic disease?
    A. Acute disease is common early in life but diminishes with age; chronic disease increases with age.
    b. Acute disease increases with age; chronic disease decreases with age.
    c. Both acute and chronic disease increase with age.
    d. Both acute and chronic disease decrease with age.

11. The biological limit of life is known technically as:
    a. life expectancy.
    B. life span.
    c. longevity.
    d. terminal drop.

12. According to contemporary researchers, which of the following is a plausible explanation of why death occurs?
    a. In every individual there is a master biological switch that prescribes the hour of death and cannot be changed or reset.
    b. Chronic disease of one sort or another is inevitable in everyone sometime in his or her lifetime.
    C. Each "system" of the body has a life of its own and the interaction of these systems determines how long a person lives.
    d. Were it not for disease, accidents, and other unpredictable influences, people would probably never die.

13. Male rhesus monkeys who lose status in their social group:
    a. secrete more testosterone, indicating that the biological clock is sensitive to social context.
    B. secrete less testosterone, indicating that the biological clock is sensitive to social context.
    c. live longer than those with higher status.
    d. live fewer years than those with higher status.

14. Concerning the relationship of the biological clock to social context, which of the following is true?
    a. There are no physical features of growing old that are not the result of disease or social context.
    b. Social context has very little effect on the physical effects of aging.
    C. The body is more likely to rust from disuse than to wear out from overuse.
    d. Exercise during late adulthood is generally not recommended.

15. Research related to the Hayflick model supports the theory:
    A. of a genetically based limit to the life of each cell.
    b. that disease, rather than genetics, determines whether cells die, or live indefinitely.
    c. that nutrition and exercise are major factors in life expectancy.
    d. that people are outliving their genetically programmed life expectancy because of improved health practices.

Essay Questions

1. Define and differentiate **biological clock, life span,** and **life expectancy.** What (if any) changes have occurred in each of these during the past century? (audio program)

2. Explain the "watch in the water" metaphor introduced in the audio program. If the biological clock is the watch, what in the water influences its operation and has an impact on older bodies? (audio program)

3. Discuss why researchers are "rewriting the book on aging and sexuality," by addressing the following questions. (audio program)

   a. Are the changes in sexual response that occur in older bodies the result of aging or chronic disease?
   b. What is the impact of social context on sexuality? How did the decision to segregate older men and women living in nursing homes lead to an erroneous conclusion regarding the biology of aging and sexuality?

4. Explain the concept of **programmed death** at the cellular level. What research evidence supports the idea of a genetically based limit to the life of a cell, and the possibility of resetting this limit? (audio program)

5. What are the typical age-related changes that occur in each of the following during late adulthood? (textbook)

   a. brain function
   b. immune system
   c. sense organs and major body systems

6. Briefly explain the following theories of aging. (textbook)

   a. the wear-and-tear theory
   b. cellular theories
   c. programmed senescence

7. The audio program points out that the decline in sexual capacity once believed to be an inevitable accompaniment to aging may depend more on social context than on the passage of time per se. What other physical changes do we often associate with aging that might be due to factors other than aging? (audio program)

8. If the biological clock can be reset, what implications will this have for life-span development in the individual? What impact do you predict it will have for society? (audio program)

9. What is meant by the "squaring of the pyramid?" What are some of the social problems that experts predict will be the result of this trend? (textbook)

10. Do you believe that ageist stereotypes of late adulthood are declining, increasing, or unlikely to change? Explain your reasoning. (textbook)

References

Finch, Caleb E. and Schneider, Edward L. (1985). *Handbook of the biology of aging.* New York: Van Nostrand Reinhold.

This work is considered a definitive source for research on aging.

Late Adulthood: Cognitive Development

AUDIO PROGRAM: The Trees and the Forest

OVERVIEW

If each season of life has its own gift of knowledge, what is the gift of late adulthood? This question is explored in the audio program "The Trees and the Forest," and in Chapter 24 of *The Developing Person Through the Life Span, 2/e.* As more and more people reach their 60s, 70s, 80s, and beyond, this question becomes of more and more practical significance.

Cross-sectional research finds that on almost any measure of cognitive functioning people older than age 60 do worse than younger people. But how should these findings be interpreted? As Kathleen Berger notes in the textbook, "one of the pitfalls for the psychologist dealing with the elderly . . . is that he or she may measure the behavior of the elderly by standards that are largely irrelevant to the elderly themselves." Indeed, tests of intellectual functioning typically reward speed in performance—which declines with age (Audio Program 23)—and are generally designed to test younger adults on school- or career-related skills.

Both the textbook and audio program use the **information-processing** model to organize the discussion of how memory changes in late adulthood. Despite fears fueled by increased public awareness, for must adults aging brings not a pathological loss of memory, such as the **dementia** of **Alzheimer's disease,** but a change in processing that primarily disrupts **secondary memory.** Several potential causes of this decline in secondary memory are explored in the audio program and textbook, including the possibility that disuse of this type of memory, rather than aging per se, is responsible. This echoes the "use it or lose it" theme of Lesson 23 regarding physical ability and skill in late adulthood.

Program 24 also presents psychologist Warner Schaie who discusses the cognitive changes that are likely to come with each decade after 60. Psychologist Marion Perlmutter talks about the philosophical turn of mind and **wisdom** that may be the special gift of this season of life. Many older adults seem to experience a better integration of emotion and cognition, the emergence of a more global perspective, a more fully developed aesthetic sense, deeper spiritual values, and a tendency towards reflection and **life review.** This is a valuable experience that may represent an attempt to put life into perspective, and to establish continuity with previous and subsequent generations.

LESSON GOALS

1. To explain why different measures of cognition may be needed to assess thinking in older and younger adults.

2. To apply the information-processing approach to cognition in old age.

3. To discuss the potential for new cognitive development, growth, and wisdom during late adulthood.

4. To summarize the causes and effects of the different dementias.

LESSON 24 EXERCISE: PERSONAL WISDOM IN OLDER ADULTS

A theme of both the textbook and audio program is that despite a decline in one type of memory, positive changes in intellectual functioning may be characteristic of late adulthood. Textbook author Kathleen Berger discusses the theories of Erikson, Maslow, and Neugarten regarding cognitive growth during late adulthood, while in the audio program Professor Marion Perlmutter discusses her research on the **personal wisdom** of the elderly. These researchers maintain that many people become more responsive to nature, more interested in creative endeavors, more reflective, and more philosophical as they grow older.

To examine the topic of cognitive growth in later life and the philosophical turn of mind common to this age, the exercise for Lesson 24 asks students to complete a modified version of Larry Bugen's "Life/Values/Goals Inventory." Bugen's questionnaire focuses on the ways in which an individual's awareness of his or her own mortality influences values, goals, and attitudes towards life. Older students are asked to answer the questions from two life-cycle perspectives: as they felt during early or middle adulthood; and as they feel now, during later adulthood. Younger students are asked to have an older adult whom they know well complete the questionnaire from these two perspectives.

After the student (or the student's subject) completes the questionnaire, he or she is to interpret their (or their subject's) responses by answering three questions. His or her answers to *these* questions, and not the actual questionnaire, are to be returned to the instructor.

As a follow-up to this exercise, the instructor could prepare a summary of students' responses, focusing on the extent to which they concur with points made in the textbook and audio program regarding cognitive growth in late adulthood. For example, did the values and/or goals of older adults (question 1) differ from those of younger adults? Were there differences in the extent to which younger and older adults' lifestyles (question 2) reflected these values? As an alternative, the instructor could ask each student to reflect further on his or her own cognitive development by telling what he or she has learned from this lesson, or how the lesson's content has personal meaning to him or her.

AUDIO TESTBANK

Note: A testbank for the text is published separately by Worth Publishers, Inc.

Multiple Choice Questions

The correct answer to each question is identified by a capital letter.

1. Imagery, rhymes, context cues, and acronyms to assist in remembering are examples of:
   a. sensory register.
   b. primary memory.
   C. encoding strategies.
   d. retrieval strategies.

2. According to the information-processing model of memory, which type of memory is most likely to decline during late adulthood?
   a. primary memory
   B. secondary memory
   c. tertiary memory
   d. sensory memory

3. What explanation of this memory decline is offered in the audio program?
   a. Most older adults have difficulty paying attention long enough to memorize.
   b. By the time a person is in his or her 60s or 70s, a sufficient number of nerve cells have died to disrupt the easy formation of new memories.
   C. Older adults do not automatically use the best strategies of encoding and retrieving information.
   d. All of these explanations were offered as reasons for memory decline.

4. Which type of material would a person in his or her 70s probably have the greatest difficulty remembering?
   a. the dates of birth of family members
   b. a phone number given by the telephone operator
   C. phone numbers of former business clients
   d. the first house they lived in

5. Remembering a phone number that you just looked up long enough to dial it requires the use of:
   a. sensory register.
   B. primary memory.
   c. secondary memory.
   d. tertiary memory.

6. Concerning the public's fear of Alzheimer's disease, which of the following is true?
   a. A serious loss of memory, such as that occurring in people with Alzheimer's disease, can be expected by most people once they reach their 60s.
   B. Of people over age 65, at most 5 percent of the population is affected by conditions such as Alzheimer's disease.
   c. Alzheimer's disease is much more common today than it was 50 years ago.
   d. Alzheimer's disease is less common today than it was 50 years ago.

7. At the present stage of research into cognitive development during late adulthood, which of the following statements has the greatest support?
   a. There is uniform decline in all stages of memory during late adulthood.
   b. Tertiary memory shows the greatest decline with age.
   c. Primary memory shows the greatest decline with age.
   D. The decline in memory may be the result of the failure to use effective encoding and retrieval strategies.

8. The stages of memory are in order of duration from briefest to longest-lasting:
   a. secondary memory; primary memory; tertiary memory.
   b. primary memory; tertiary memory; secondary memory.
   c. tertiary memory; primary memory; secondary memory.
   D. primary memory; secondary memory; tertiary memory.

9. Seventy-five-year-old Lena has vivid memories of her childhood experiences on the family farm. This type of memory is called:
   a. sensory register.
   b. primary memory.
   C. tertiary memory.
   d. secondary memory.

10. The aspect of memory that involves remembering by pulling information out of memory is called:
    a. encoding.
    B. retrieval.
    c. sensory register.
    d. primary memory.

11. New cognitive development during late adulthood is characterized by what Professor Marion Perlmutter refers to as:
    a. dementia.
    b. tertiary memory.
    C. wisdom.
    d. encoding.

12. Memories that are in our minds over the intermediate term, but not consciously in awareness, constitute:
    a. sensory register.
    b. primary memory.
    C. secondary memory.
    d. tertiary memory.

13. Being in the same context in which a memory was originally stored:
    A. often facilitates retrieval.
    b. often disrupts retrieval.
    c. usually has no effect on retrieval.
    d. often facilitates encoding.

14. Professor Schaie's study of intellectual change in late adulthood is based on retesting the same individuals periodically and adding a fresh sample of people each time. This method of research is called:
    a. longitudinal research.
    b. cross-sectional research.
    C. sequential research.
    d. empirical research.

15. Research on cognitive development during late adulthood has shown that:
    A. there are enormous individual differences in ability.
    b. very few people function as well cognitively at age 60 as they did in their 50s.
    c. once people retire, cognitive decline is inevitable.
    d. sequential research gives a misleading picture of intellectual change during late adulthood.

Essay Questions

1. Discuss how the focus of the study of intelligence in older persons has changed in recent years. (audio program)

2. Describe each of the following memory stages and whether the function of each stage normally changes as an individual ages. (audio program)
    a. primary memory
    b. secondary memory
    c. tertiary memory

3. Describe the normal changes in intellectual functioning that occur in most persons during their 60s, 70s, and 80s. (audio program)

4. In terms of the information-processing model, how are input, storage, and program affected by age? (textbook)

5. Discuss the relationship of health and education to the age-related decline in cognitive functioning. (textbook)

6. Explain why the typical memory experiment is often biased against the elderly person. (textbook)

7. Describe several of the positive cognitive developments that are likely to find expression during late adulthood. (textbook)

8. Imagine that you have been asked to develop a new test of cognitive functioning specifically for adults over the age of 65. What abilities do you think should be tested? What kinds of questions would you include? Why? (audio program and textbook)

9. Your 70-year-old mother seems to be forgetting things much more than she did a few years ago, before she retired from her career as an accountant. She is concerned that she is developing Alzheimer's disease. How would you go about determining whether her memory loss is a result of disuse rather than disease? (audio program and textbook)

10. Discuss the special wisdom of late adulthood. What cognitive changes do psychologists believe that it brings? Why do you believe that this gift occurs during this final season of life? (audio program and textbook)

References

Perlmutter, M. and List, J. A. (1982). Learning in later adulthood. In T. M. Field, A. Huston, H. C. Quay, L. Troll, and G. E. Finley (eds.), *Review of human development*. New York: Wiley.

Psychologist Marion Perlmutter, who is introduced in the audio program, offers a lucid critique of laboratory research on cognitive development during late adulthood.

Averyt, A., Furst, E., and Hummel, D. D. (1987). *Successful aging: A sourcebook for older people and their families.* New York: Ballantine.

Written in a sprightly but matter-of-fact tone, this book is a useful resource for the older adult and the developmentalist. In addition to dispelling a number of myths of aging, it discusses such major topics as Alzheimer's disease, alcoholism, divorce, and death.

Late Adulthood: Psychosocial Development

OVERVIEW

Lesson 25 completes the series' examination of late adulthood by asking, "How is psychosocial development affected by old age?" Chapter 25 of *The Developing Person Through the Life Span, 2/e,* explores **disengagement, activity,** and **continuity-discontinuity theories,** emphasizing that the diversity of developmental patterns during late adulthood is not adequately explained by any single theory. A look at the ways in which the elderly meet their need for affiliation follows. For most people during this season of life, their **social convoy** of family and friends is central to their happiness.

In Audio Program 25 the listener meets three very different grandparents whose stories address three questions: What is the right age to become a grandparent? How has the dramatic rise in divorce rates since the 1960s affected the relationships of grandparents with their children and grandchildren? What are the effects on grandparenting of the increase in life expectancy during this century?

Developmentalist Linda Burton has found that those who become grandparents during their 40s or 50s ("on time" grandparents) are generally happier and better prepared than those who have the grandparenting role thrust on them earlier.

In discussing the effects of rising divorce rates on grandparents, sociologist Andrew Cherlin notes that grandparental ties are normally weakened on the father's side and strengthened on the mother's side because custody of children is usually awarded to the mother.

The increased life expectancy of people in this century means that most grandparents can now expect to spend an entire career—as much as one-half of their lives—with their grandchildren. In the audio program, Professor Cherlin outlines three stages of grandparenthood.

Although being a grandparent has changed in response to patterns of divorce, longevity, and timing, it retains a central role in the psychosocial development of many individuals during late adulthood. As author Kathleen Berger notes, "when the bond is close between grandparents and grandchildren, both generations are likely to benefit." The program concludes with the speculation that in the future the role of grandparents may become greater than ever.

LESSON GOALS

1. To discuss the impact of grandparenthood on the individual and the family.

2. To discuss how being a grandparent has changed during the past century.

3. To consider the psychosocial development of older persons from a variety of theoretical perspectives, while recognizing the diversity of their individual experiences.

4. To describe the special problems that face some older adults in contemporary America, including adjustment to retirement, frail health, poverty, changing relationships, and widowhood.

LESSON 25 EXERCISE: GRANDPARENTS

In applying this lesson to their own lives, students are asked to reflect on the changing role of grandparents by writing answers to several questions.

As a follow-up to this exercise, the instructor could prepare a summary of students' responses, focusing on the extent to which they concur with points made in the textbook and program regarding the changing nature of grandparenthood over time. For example, is there evidence of greater "non-interference" between grandparents and grandchildren today? Are grandparents today more likely to be fun-loving, indulgent playmates than the family matriarchs or patriarchs of previous generations? Are there consistent differences in the grandparenting styles of grandmothers and grandfathers? Do styles of grandparenting vary based on ethnic background? If this exercise coincides with a class meeting, encouraging students to share their recollections of their grandparents should lead to an interesting class discussion.

AUDIO TESTBANK

Note: A testbank for the text is published separately by Worth Publishers, Inc.

Multiple Choice Questions

The correct answer to each question is identified by a capital letter.

1. During the second half of the 20th century, the clocks that govern grandparenthood are running:
   a. for a shorter period of time than in the past.
   B. for a longer period of time than in the past.
   c. for about the same amount of time as in the past.
   d. for a shorter period of time than in the past, but at a faster rate.

2. Which of the following is *not* one of the changes in grandparenting that has occurred during this century?
   a. Most grandparents are better off financially than in the past.
   b. Grandparents can expect to have more years with their grandchildren than in the past.

C. The average age of grandparents when the first grandchild is born has decreased.

d. Most grandparents are no longer having children of their own when their first grandchild is born.

3. Rachel became a grandmother when she was 31 years old. Based on research findings concerning the age at which one becomes a grandparent, which of the following will probably characterize Rachel's situation?

    a. Being "on-time," Rachel will probably adapt easily to the role of grandparent.

    B. Rachel will probably be less happy with the role of grandparent than she would be if it had occurred during her 40s or 50s.

    c. Whether a grandparent will adapt easily to his or her new role is difficult to determine based on his or her age.

    d. All of the above will characterize Rachel's situation.

4. Jim and Mary's son recently became divorced. What effect will this most likely have on their relationship to their son's children?

    a. Their grandparental ties will probably strengthen.

    b. Divorce will probably not affect this relationship.

    C. Their grandparental ties will probably weaken.

    d. The children's relationship with their grandparents on the father's side will become stronger.

5. The overall relationship between grandparents and grandchildren is usually:

    a. closest when the grandchildren are of preschool age.

    b. weakened when grandchildren are adolescents.

    c. strengthened when grandchildren become adults themselves.

    D. characterized by all of the above statements.

6. Compared to grandparents, great-grandparents:

    A. are less likely to be involved in a "hands-on" way with their great-grandchildren.

    b. are more likely to spoil their great-grandchildren.

    c. are usually stricter with their great-grandchildren.

    d. report weaker feelings of love for their great-grandchildren.

7. Experts predict that in the future the importance of the grandparent in most families will:

    a. decrease as ties weaken due to rising divorce rates.

    b. remain about the same as it is now.

    C. increase as the typical grandparent will have more time, more resources, and fewer grandchildren.

    d. depend on the degree to which the current trend of grandparents to "distance" themselves from grandchildren continues.

8. Today, one out of every _____ marriages is likely to end in divorce.

    A. two

    b. three

    c. four

    d. five

9. Which of the following best describes how a grandparent's relationship to his or her grandchild typically changes as the grandchild moves from childhood, through adolescence, to adulthood?
   a. The relationship usually becomes increasingly closer as the grandchild matures.
   b. The relationship usually becomes weaker and weaker as the grandchild matures.
   C. The relationship is strongest during childhood, weakens during adolescence, but often becomes close again when the grandchild becomes an adult.
   d. None of the above; there is virtually no predictability in the grandparent-grandchild relationship.

10. Since the beginning of this century, the average age at which people become grandparents has:
    a. increased.
    b. decreased.
    C. not changed.
    d. become completely unpredictable.

11. Concerning the impact that the timing of grandparenthood has on the grandparent, which of the following is true?
    a. Generally speaking, the younger the person is when he or she becomes a grandparent, the better the adjustment to the role.
    B. Because grandparenting is a role that someone else decides for you, its timing can have a major psychological impact.
    c. The timing of grandparenthood is of relatively little significance in its impact.
    d. All of the above are true.

12. When their children divorce, grandparents typically find that their relationships with grandchildren become:
    A. stronger on the mother's side and weaker on the father's.
    b. stronger on both the mother's and father's sides.
    c. weaker on the mother's side and stronger on the father's.
    d. weaker on both the mother's and father's sides.

13. Which of the following was *not* suggested in the program as a reason that the great-grandparent–great-grandchild relationship usually is not as close as the grandparent–grandchild relationship?
    a. There are too many layers of family in between great-grandparents and great-grandchildren.
    b. Because of their advanced age, great-grandparents are not as interested in helping out as much.
    C. Great-grandparents often resent the encroachment of the great-grandchild on their relationships with grandchildren.
    d. The generation gap between great-grandparents and great-grandchildren is often accompanied by differences in styles of child-rearing.

14. According to information presented in the audio program, most grand-parents:
   a. wish for less independence and a greater role in the lives of their children and grandchildren.
   b. feel that their grandchildren are brought up too permissively.
   C. struggle to balance their desire for independent living with a desire to have a strong role in the lives of their children and grandchildren.
   d. feel resentful of the "norm of noninterference."

15. When grandchildren become adults, their relationship to their grandparents often:
   a. becomes a source of frustration and resentment.
   b. ends, because of their own family and career obligations.
   C. becomes closer and more loving than when they were children.
   d. becomes a source of conflict with their parents.

Essay Questions

1. Discuss the impact of being an "on-time" or "off-time" grandparent. (audio program)

2. Discuss how grandparents are affected by the divorce of their children. What effect does divorce usually have on grandparental ties on the mother's side? On the father's side? (audio program)

3. Describe the three phases of grandparenting. How does the grandparent's relationship to the grandchildren change during these phases? (audio program)

4. Describe the psychosocial development of older adults as interpreted by the following theories. (textbook)

   a. disengagement theory
   b. activity theory
   c. continuity–discontinuity theory

5. Cite several ways in which retirement has changed for many contemporary Americans. (textbook)

6. Discuss the importance of friendship and the social convoy to the well-being of older people. (textbook)

7. Describe some of the typical changes in the quality of marriage that occur during late adulthood. (textbook)

8. As a family counselor, you are asked to discuss the joys and pains of grandparenthood with a group of new grandparents. Outline a counseling program that would promote their adjustment to their new roles as grand-parents and increase their understanding of what to expect of their relation-ship with their grandchildren as they and their grandchildren get older. (audio program)

9. The audio program indicates that grandparental ties typically weaken following divorce on the father's side of the family, and strengthen following divorce on the mother's side. If this is true, and present trends in divorce continue, what will be the impact on the "typical American family?" On society as a whole? (audio program)

10. Speculate about how your role as a grandparent might differ from the role played by your great-great-grandparents. (audio program and textbook)

References

Cherlin, A., and Furstenberg, F. (1986). *The new American grandparent.* New York: Basic Books.

Professor Andrew Cherlin, who is heard on the audio program, discusses the changing role of grandparents in contemporary society.

Death and Dying

AUDIO PROGRAM: Of Seasons and Survivors

OVERVIEW

The final lesson of *Seasons of Life* explores the changing meanings of death and dying in our culture. As discussed in the textbook assignment, many experts believe that accepting death is the final step in a fully lived life. In the contemporary Western world, however, death is increasingly removed from everyday life and concealed through the institutionalization of the dying. This denial of death has been accompanied by a decrease in the number of "good deaths"— those that are swift, dignified, and in the presence of family members—as the medical community continues to discover new ways of sustaining life. Consistent with this recent cultural trend to deny death, the open practice of grieving has declined, often resulting in a crippling effect on the lives of the bereaved.

Chapter 26 of *The Developing Person Through the Life Span, 2/e,* discusses several other issues regarding death and dying, including the pivotal work of Elizabeth Kübler-Ross, whose interviews with dying patients helped make professionals and the public more aware of the specific experiences and needs of the dying. Two controversial topics that are addressed are the **hospice** as an alternative living arrangement for those who are terminally ill and the practice of euthanasia.

Audio Program 26, "Of Seasons and Survivors," focuses on the stories of two deaths and their impacts on surviving family members. The listener discovers that losing a loved one "in season," at the end of a long, full life, has a very different meaning than losing a loved one unexpectedly, and "out of season," when he or she is in the prime of life. The sudden death of a person who is not "supposed" to die, such as the young man in the audio program, is most difficult to bear. Surviving family members may be tormented by conflicting emotions of guilt, denial, anger, and sorrow. Having time to anticipate the death does not necessarily reduce the pain of loss, but it can lessen the conflicting feelings that survivors experience regarding the death and allow family members to come together with the dying person and share their affection for one another.

Expert commentary in the program is provided by psychologist Camille Wortman who has studied the grieving process extensively. Professor Wortman discusses several common misconceptions about the process of grieving and offers a number of practical "do's and don'ts" for those who would comfort the bereaved.

LESSON GOALS

1. To discuss our culture's attitudes toward death and dying and how these affect the process of adjusting to bereavement.

2. To identify factors that can make dying an easier process and bereavement less traumatic for survivors.

3. To discuss death as a way of giving meaning to life and as a necessary part of the developmental process.

4. To contrast the impact of an "in-season" death with an "out-of-season" death on surviving family members.

LESSON 26 EXERCISE: COPING WITH DEATH AND DYING

To stimulate students' thinking about some of the issues raised by the text and audio program concerning death and dying, the exercise for Lesson 26 requires them to prepare brief answers to several questions.

The issues addressed by the questions include the importance of rituals in mourning (question 1), the ways in which each person confronts his or her own impending death (question 2), the cultural tendency to deny death (question 3), developmental shifts in the way death is viewed (question 4), the "do's and don'ts" of comforting those who are bereaved (question 5), and the controversial issues of euthanasia and the hospice approach to dying patients (question 6).

Completing this exercise should help students to integrate the material with their own feelings. If there is enough diversity in the ages and/or ethnic backgrounds of students, this exercise might also allow the instructor to illustrate cohort effects in attitudes toward death and dying.

AUDIO TESTBANK

Note: A testbank for the text is published separately by Worth Publishers, Inc.

Multiple Choice Questions

The correct answer to each question is identified by a capital letter.

1. In her research with bereaved families, Professor Wortman found that:
   a. most people fully recovered from the loss of a loved one.
   B. many people were permanently changed by the loss of a loved one.
   c. after about 5 years, fewer than 25 percent of the people studied had frequent thoughts about their lost loved one.
   d. because they denied their grief, those who returned quickly to their normal routines took longer to recover.

2. Compared to previous periods in history, death today is more likely to occur:
   A. "in season," after a long life.
   b. "out of season," due to the higher incidence of accidents, heart disease, and cancer.
   c. in any season of life, as a result of its greater unpredictability.
   d. swiftly and with greater dignity.

3. Professor Wortman's research with bereaved families indicates that a common misconception regarding bereavement is the belief that:
   a. those who have lost a loved one want to forget about their loss as soon as possible.
   b. men are better able to "bear up" to grief than are women.
   C. people are able to break completely their attachments to lost loved ones.
   d. most bereaved persons do not want others to know of their emotional turmoil.

4. Harriet's husband Fred died two years ago. Harriet still thinks about Fred every day and often has imaginary conversations with him, in which she imagines how he might have dealt with a certain problem. Sometimes Harriet becomes concerned that she is losing her mind and not recovering from her loss. Professor Wortman's research would indicate that:
   a. Harriet's inability to let go of Fred is unhealthy and that she should seek professional counseling.
   b. Harriet should force herself to stop thinking about Fred.
   c. Harriet most likely never developed a sense of identity that was independent of her husband.
   D. such thoughts, feelings, and attachments are perfectly normal among people who have lost a loved one.

5. In seeking to comfort a grieving friend, it is a good idea to:
   a. try and provide a philosophical perspective on the loss.
   b. encourage the person to get back to their normal routine as quickly as possible.
   C. let the person know that if they want to talk about their grief, you are available at any time.
   d. encourage the person to "bear up" and not give in to self-indulgent feelings of grief.

6. Professor Wortman's research has indicated that recovery from grief is greatly facilitated when the bereaved person:
   A. has some form of religious faith.
   b. refuses to allow grief to overcome them.
   c. is well-educated and employed full-time.
   d. turns their sorrow or anger into positive energy expressed in a new hobby, career, or relationship.

7. Based on the two deaths described in the audio program, which of the following is true?
   a. It may be more difficult to accept and recover from an out-of-season death of a loved one than an in-season death.
   b. It may be more difficult to accept and recover from an unexpected death than from a death that is anticipated.
   c. The impact of a loved one's death on surviving family members depends partly on whether the death occurred in the prime of life or at the end of a long life.
   D. All of the above are true.

8. Which of the following statements would probably *not* be helpful to a bereaved person?
   a. "Everyone dies sooner or later."
   b. "God must have needed him or her for another purpose."
   c. "Be strong, everyone must cope with death."
   D. None of the above would be helpful.

9. In her studies of people who had lost a spouse or child 4 to 7 years earlier, Professor Wortman found that the majority of people:
   a. were still having difficulties coping with their grief.
   b. still thought about their loved one daily.
   c. had painful memories that they were unable to shut out.
   D. experienced all of the above reactions to the death.

10. Jack's wife recently died after a sudden illness. Jack's recovery would probably be helped the most:
   a. if he quickly remarried.
   b. if he moved to a new city, took a new job, and made a clean break with his past.
   C. by sharing his feelings with a friend who has experienced a similar loss.
   d. by all of the above suggestions.

11. A common misconception about the grieving process is that:
   A. after a year or two people fully recover from their loss.
   b. those in grief will never fully recover.
   c. those in grief should be left alone.
   d. people should not be hurried through their grief.

12. For Dorothy and Dick Taylor, whose son was killed in an automobile accident, an important factor in their recovery from grief was:
   a. their having another child.
   B. their religious faith.
   c. their quick return to a normal routine.
   d. their moving to a new community.

13. In the audio program it was suggested that the legacy of Sarkis Hashoian's death differs from that of Richard Taylor's death because:
   a. Sarkis Hashoian died "out of season."
   b. Richard Taylor died "in season."
   c. Sarkis Hashoian had fewer relatives.
   D. Sarkis Hashoian died "in season."

14. In her research with bereaved families, Professor Wortman found that:
   a. women tended to grieve for longer periods than men.
   b. men tended to grieve for longer periods than women.
   C. people often remained attached to their lost loved ones for years.
   d. people tended to break their attachments to lost loved ones sooner when the loss occurred "out of season."

15. An important message of the audio program, "Of Seasons and Survivors," is that:
    A. most people misunderstand the process of grief.
    b. those in grief tend to dwell too much on their loss.
    c. the ritualization of death in funerals, wakes, etc., is not helpful to those in grief.
    d. all of the above are true.

Essay Questions

1. Identify two misunderstandings the general public has about the grieving process. (audio program)

2. Describe two ways in which well-intentioned persons are often unhelpful to those who are grieving. (audio program)

3. Explain how people *can* be helpful to those who have lost a loved one and identify other factors that facilitate the recovery process. (audio program)

4. Contrast the impact of "in-season" and "out-of-season" deaths on surviving family members. (audio program)

5. Describe the five emotional stages a dying person goes through in dealing with imminent death, as described by Elizabeth Kübler-Ross. (textbook)

6. Outline the four stages of mourning. (textbook)

7. Discuss several ways modern culture has made coping with death and bereavement more difficult than it was in the past. (textbook)

8. Discuss the concept of a "good death" and explain some of the ways in which the dying have been helped to achieve a good death. (textbook)

9. Discuss the pros and cons of the hospice as an alternative living arrangement for terminally ill patients. (textbook)

10. Discuss how people's views of death change over the life span, and some of the factors that influence the meaning of death for them. (textbook)

References

Birren, James and Schaie, K. Warner (1985). *Handbook of the psychology of aging.* New York: Van Nostrand Rhinehold.

This excellent handbook provides overviews of the theory and research relevant to numerous issues concerning aging.

The Television Term Project

The Television Term Project consists of 25 essay questions that students are to complete any time during the course. The questions are meant to guide students' viewing of the television programs and to serve as a final project that integrates the various components of the *Seasons of Life* telecourse.

Questions 1–20 are grouped into five sets of four questions each, each set of questions corresponding to each television program. Many of the questions are similar from program to program and will help students make meaningful connections between the programs and their own life experiences. Other questions focus on important developmental themes of the series, such as how the events of a particular stage of life are affected by those that come before and affects those that follow.

Questions 21–25 represent a summing up of the content of the *Seasons of Life* telecourse and are therefore to be completed after all five programs have been viewed. The questions encourage students to think about the life cycle as a whole, rather than as a collection of separate stages. Several of the questions are concerned with major themes of the series, including how the life story evolves, the increasing developmental diversity that occurs as people age, and the relative control exerted by each of the three developmental clocks at various ages.

In some cases, students are given a choice between questions for younger and older students. They are encouraged to answer the questions that seem better suited to them. Once they have answered all 25 questions, students are directed to send their entire set of answers to their instructor.

The manner in which completed Television Term Projects are evaluated and the type of feedback provided to students are determined by the individual instructor. Answers to questions that deal more directly than others with factual program content—questions 2, 8, 11, 15, 19, 23, and 25, for example—should be checked for accuracy to make sure that students have grasped the central concepts of each program.

For most of the term project questions, there are no simple correct or incorrect answers, however. These questions require that students reflect on issues and stories depicted in the series, often integrating this information with their own life experiences. The evaluation and feedback provided for these questions should naturally follow the guidelines by which the instructor evaluates each lesson's exercise and similar projects in other courses. Some instructors find it useful to assign points for various elements of a paper or project, including its interest level and creativity; how clearly it focuses on important facts, examples, and accurate principles of human development drawn from the various components of the telecourse; and whether the writing is logical and well-organized.

Finally, it should be noted that in the term project instructions students are encouraged to watch the television programs with other students in the course, family, or friends. They also are encouraged to discuss the questions with other people to help clarify their understanding and to benefit from others' perspectives on issues raised in the programs. The Television Term Project is intended to create a learning experience and not to serve as a final examination.